Co-mediation:

Using a psychological, paired approach to resolving conflict

Editor: Monica Hanaway

© Monica Hanaway 2012

Co-mediation:
using a psychological paired approach
to resolving conflict

ISBN: 978-0-9571713-0-5

Published by Corporate Harmony
Whitehouse
Peppard Lane
Henley-on-Thames
Oxon, RG9 1NG

Book designed by Michael Walsh at
The Better Book Company
5 Lime Close • Chichester PO19 6SW

and privately printed by
ImprintDigital.net
Seychelles Farm • Upton Pyne • Exeter • Devon EX5 5HY

CONTENTS

Part 3: Different co-mediation models

AUTHORS

MONICA HANAWAY is an accredited mediator, psychotherapist, supervisor, business coach, stress management consultant and management and leadership trainer. She is deputy course leader for the Diploma in Existential Coaching at the Existential Academy and lecturer and supervisor on doctorate programmes at the New School of Psychotherapy and Counselling Psychology (NSPC), Academic supervisor for Oxford University MSc Psychotherapy programes, Senior Lecturer on Mediation Courses at the School of Psychotherapy and Counselling Psychology (SPCP) and Webster Graduate Business School at Regent's College, London, visiting lecturer in mediation at Riga Graduate School of Law, and in Organisational Psychology at King's College, London.

She has worked for many years as a coach and consultant to senior staff in the public and private sectors and has over 20 years' experience as a Senior Manager, strategist and policy maker.

She has mediated in a wide variety of disputes involving Commercial, Employment and Workplace disputes, Family conflicts, disputes between young people, including gangs, as well as Restorative Justice work with victims and perpetrators of crime. She also works with global corporate companies as a consultant and coach in leadership skills and conflict management.

She is Co-Director of The CH Group. The company provides coaching, mediation and training to a diverse client group in both private and public sectors, and in the community and holds contracts for providing mediation to some global EAP companies.

She is currently working on a book entitled 'Why people say No – THE question for Unlocking Conflict and Finding

Resolution' and co-editing a book with Emmy van Deurzen on Existential Coaching due to be published by Palgrave in May 2012

TRICIA HAYES is a mediator who always works as part of a co-mediating team (of two). She began her mediating career as a volunteer community mediator and went on to train and supervise others in the service. She holds a psychology degree and a postgraduate certificate (PGCE) in adult education. She is a member of the Mediators Institute of Ireland (MII) and completed her masters in mediation and conflict resolution in 2006 in UCD.

JUDITH MCKIMM-VORDERWINKLER is an independent mediator and member of the ONE~resolve mediation group. Her visual communication background, multicultural experience, and fluency in six languages has led her to specialize in intercultural communication. She holds a Master's degree in Intercultural Studies.

DIANA MITCHELL is a UKCP registered psychotherapist, a clinical supervisor and accredited mediator. Most of her mediation work has been time-limited workplace mediations where she either mediates on her own or with another mediator. She is a lecturer on the School of Psychotherapy and Counselling Psychology five-day intensive ADR mediation course at Regent's College in London and also gives regular seminars on mediation for the Webster Graduate School at Regent's College. As a member of The CH Group she has participated in mediations and workshops with Monica Hanaway and Jamie Reed.

MARY LOU O'KENNEDY is a mediator, conflict management coach and trainer in the field of mediation and conflict coaching. She has over twenty years experience in management in the private and local development sector in Ireland. She holds a Masters in social work from the University of Pittsburgh, USA where she acted as a researcher and contributing author to a book 'Social Work Intervention in an Economic Crisis' edited by Martha Baum and Pamela Twiss. She has lectured in Sociology at degree level with the Institute of Adult Education and is currently a trainer in the CINERGY® Model of Conflict Management Coaching and in Mediation. Mary Lou is a practitioner member of the Mediators Institute of Ireland serving as Council member and Chairperson of its Education Committee from 2009 to 2011. She is a co-founder of Amicus Mediation Ltd in which she has practiced the use of the co-mediation model mediating and coaching over the past five years in private companies, the public sector, communities and families.

PHIL O'HEHIR is a solicitor, now working full time as a mediator. Phil is a director of Amicus Mediation Limited and trains and coaches in the CINERGY™ model of conflict management coaching. She has provided coaching and mediation services to public sector organisations including Local Authorities; the Health Services; the Department of Education as well as the Community and Private sectors, including legal practices. She is a member of the Mediator's Institute of Ireland, the Irish Commercial Mediator's Association and the Law Society of Ireland.

PAUL RANDOLPH is an Accredited Mediator (CEDR June 1999 and SPC: May 2000), and a Barrister, called in 1971. He practises from the Field Court Chambers, Gray's Inn, London. He is Course Leader and Lecturer on a Mediation Course at the School of Psychotherapy and Counselling Psychology (SPCP), Regent's College, London, which trains and accredits mediators. He is a member of the

UK Bar Council ADR Committee, a Board member of the Civil Mediation Council, and is on the London County Court Mediation Committee. He was an External Examiner on Mediation at Cardiff University Law School and has for two years co-chaired the National Mediation Helpline Provider's Forum. He is Chair of LADR (Lamb Building ADR), a group of barrister mediators. He specialises in Commercial and Contractual claims, Employment and Workplace disputes, Commercial and Family Property conflicts, as well as Personal Injury and Professional Negligence claims. Paul Randolph is a highly experienced mediator, trainer, lecturer and author. He has mediated in a wide variety of disputes involving Commercial and Contractual claims, Employment and Workplace disputes, Commercial and Family Property.

JAMIE REED is an existential psychotherapist, coach, mediator and mental performance sports coach. Over the course of the last ten years he has worked in a number of different settings including primary care, private practice, employee assistance, private companies, universities and with athletes in training for competition. He is the Co-Director of The CH Group comprising Community Harmony and Corporate Harmony Limited. The company provides coaching, training and mediation services in the UK and Europe. He is a visiting tutor of mediation at Regents College School of Psychotherapy and Counselling and Webster University. He is a contributing author to a forthcoming book on Existential Perspectives on Coaching.

FOREWORD

In my various professional roles I have often worked with people in conflict. I have worked on the streets with gangs and with people suffering from homelessness and substance abuse, whose lifestyles brought them into conflict with each other and other members of the community. As a psychotherapist I have worked with families and couples who are in conflict with each other, with individuals whose conflicts with others had bought them to therapy and those clients engaged in internal conflicts with themselves. As a senior manager and leader I was often placed in the position of having to take part in disciplinary procedures, many of which seemed to have come about as the result of lack of communication and which I believed could have been avoided through earlier intervention.

In the 1990s I began to hear more about mediation and was interested to see what it might bring to the areas I was working in. I discovered a course in ADR (Alternative Dispute Resolution) run at Regent's College London and accredited by the Law Society and Bar Council, which used existential philosophy and psychology as a framework to teach mediation. I was immediately attracted to this as it drew on the same philosophical approach as my training in psychotherapy.

The course explored how the building of rapport and a working alliance, concern for the parties self-esteem, the increasing understanding of one's own and others worldviews and the importance of value systems and coping strategies lay at the heart of successful mediation.

I wasn't disappointed in the course and after qualifying I was invited to join the faculty and I continue to work as senior tutor on the course. Initially students were almost exclusively barristers, lawyers and judges. Over time, things have changed considerably and now half come from other disciplines, (e.g. therapy, human resources, management consultancy, educational, social, health and community work) where increased prominence is being given to the development of conflict resolution skills, emotional literacy and resilience. All the students learn to mediate as a sole mediator but many have asked for more information about co-mediation and how it works and so this book has been partly written with those students and graduates in mind.

In 2008, together with Jamie Reed, (a graduate of the Regent's course and contributing author), we set up Corporate Harmony Ltd (The CH Group) to provide mediation, training and conflict coaching. The company uses a co-mediation approach where two mediators work together with the parties in dispute. The CH approach is one in which the co-mediators are equals and remain together throughout the process.

As the reader will discover, there are a number of different co-mediation models. We have drawn on the experience of a number of mediators who have come from different qualification routes. Contributors have a very different personality and their writing styles reflect this. I have not tried to alter individual styles, believing it more important to retain the author's worldview and expressive style. I hope this retains the authenticity of each voice and acts as a demonstration that different styles can co-exist within the same book just as different individuals can work together as co-mediators. What we all share is the fact that although some of us may at times mediate alone, we enjoy working with a co-mediator and believe that to do so adds value and a broader dimension to the mediation process.

We begin by firstly considering what we mean when we speak of a mediation approach which is informed by psychological knowledge. The Regent's course is unique in placing this at the centre of the course and there are many training courses in mediation where the focus is on the process of obtaining a settlement, rather than the need to start with some psychological understanding of ourselves as mediators and of the individuals in the dispute. This psychological approach is used when a sole mediator is involved but becomes even more important when co-mediating as the psychological dynamics of the co-mediators' working relationship is added into the mix.

In the next chapter we offer a brief history of co-mediation so that we can set the process in context. Tricia Hayes draws on the research she undertook for her Master's thesis to look at the origins of the term co-mediation, how the mediation literature presents it, how it manifests in practice and the potential it holds.

This is followed in **Part One** by the exploration of some of the philosophical aspects which come into play in the mediation process and which are encountered when co-mediating. This includes looking at the very highly visible aspects of the co-mediation relationship and what it conveys to those observing it.

I begin by looking at the way in which the mediators' neutrality and the ability to form a respectful and trusting relationship with **each** party lies at the heart of the mediation process. Building this trusting working alliance calls for an existentially informed approach to be present not only in the work with the parties in dispute but to also be present in the relationship between mediator and co-mediator. Conflict is part of all relationships and the fact that one person is the mediator and the other the co-mediator could lead to hidden and unexpressed conflicts within the relationship. I draw on experiences of working without a co-mediator, with a less experienced co-mediator and as a co-mediator with a more experienced mediator to explore in a very practical way how existential philosophy is brought into play.

Conflicts often ensue when we experience others as different to ourselves. In this chapter I also take a brief look at the way in which the 'opponent' in a dispute takes on an alien aspect and we struggle to find connection with them. This sense of 'otherness' is often experienced as scary and negative e.g. Lacan's 'Other' or Jung's 'Darkness'. Co-mediators, through their facilitation of a dispute, show how using two different perspectives on the dispute can be creative. The co-mediators may well see things differently from each other, they may overtly disagree, but their differences are used to add richness to the resolution. The chapter seeks to explore the concept of 'otherness' and the fear and anger this can produce whilst showing the positive, creative side of being 'other' and of encountering and engaging with the other. In engaging with otherness, commonalities are often discovered and it is this discovery which often unlocks the conflict and allows movement towards a resolution.

Diana Mitchell then looks at ways in which co-mediation provides a model for peer supervision that takes place 'in the moment' of mediation. She explores the meaning and benefits which the process has for mediator and party alike. She also looks at the way in which co-mediators build trust in each other and with the parties and the importance of being able to live with 'uncertainty' rather than seek to make everything neat , tidy and clear.

Next, Jamie Reed suggests that for all of us, whether as students in mediation training, parties in dispute or indeed practicing mediators, we are constantly subject to an experience of the world and others which is based on the assumptions we have drawn from our personal history and subsequent values. The challenge comes when these assumptions are in conflict with our personal experience of the moment. Jamie contests that conflict brings to light a challenge to our assumptions and values, which if we are open to it, leads us to the possibility to 'unlearn' these assumptions as absolute truths and explore the possibility that we can see things from more than one perspective.

He suggests that for practicing mediators it is easy to feel that we have done our unlearning and we are mindful of the impact our assumptions have on us and our practice and that if they are owned and explored in supervision that we are doing OK. He believes that co-mediation offers a constant reminder that the work of unlearning never ends, that we must not only be mindful of our assumptions in relation to their impact on our experience of the disputants but also our experience with our co-mediator.

In **Part Two** we take a practical look at what co-mediation is and the advantages it offers to the mediation process. We explore the tensions and challenges of co-mediating in contrast to mediating alone and explore the practicalities of setting up a co-mediation practice.

Finally, in the **third and final section** we look at different models of co-mediation. As a Course Director of an established mediation training course, Paul Randolph is regularly asked by graduates to provide opportunities for them to gain experience through co-mediating with him. Graduates come from very different backgrounds (e.g. law, HR, psychotherapy etc.) and so bring with them particular approaches, some of which are very different from those embraced by the author. In this chapter he explores the challenges this brings to the author (being observed on occasion not practicing what he teaches and the embarrassment this may cause him) and the benefits to the apprentice co-mediator.

Unlike Paul, many co-mediators prefer only to work with co-mediators who they know well and work with on a regular basis. In the next chapter Phil O'Hehir and Mary Lou O'Kennedy, explore the dynamics involved in working together with someone on a regular basis – what is gained and what particular areas need care. They describe the Amicus

Private Practice Co-Mediation Model which they use in their private practice, mediating in the workplace, in commercial disputes, with separating couples and with communities. They demonstrate how their model works and the benefits of comediation for the clients and mediators alike. The authors explore why they believe working regularly with a regular co-mediator enhances the mediation process for their clients and for themselves as professionals drawing on real examples from their work.

In some long mediation processes conflict coaching is sometimes used as part of the process. In the next chapter I explore a case example, in which through unforeseen circumstances, one member of the co-mediation duo was unable to be present on the middle day of three-day mediation. I consider the tensions and challenges this can present to the co-mediation partnership. The chapter also covers the use of conflict coaching on a one to one basis as an integral part of a mediation process – how this was addressed in the case described and how coaching can take place as part of the pre or post mediation work and the potential benefits and drawbacks within a co-mediation model.

In the final chapter the author looks at co-mediation in the context of cross-cultural disputes. Judith McKimm-Vorderwinkler looks at co-mediation in cross cultural settings, where truly understanding people's worldviews can be a difficult, yet crucial issue. By its very nature, understanding one another depends not only on language but also on a series of defining cultural variables. She believes that if these variables are not understood and dealt with in an adequate manner by the co-mediator, no effective communication can take place, making it more difficult to build trust. The already existing anxiety in conflict may be aggravated, and the prospects of reaching an agreement can be diminished. A mediation setting of this kind is a typical example of a situation in which co-mediating with a colleague who is an intercultural and language specialist becomes necessary.

She looks at how the way emotions are perceived and expressed are culture-specific, and cultural variables determine people's behaviour as well as aspects of verbal and nonverbal expression. She believes that conflict styles and communication strategies are determined by one's culture, and culture, as well as identity, is strongly embedded in language – and vice-versa. She explores how resorting to a common language by non-native speakers in cross-cultural communication may falsify their message, since the common language may lack the association with their own culture, and how speaking a foreign language in an emotionally charged situation can have psycholinguistic implications which need to be understood and managed appropriately. She shows how being able to deal with these multiple factors in a mediation will ensure effective communication, allowing the building of a relationship of trust, and giving the individuals in dispute the assurance of being truly heard.

We hope that this book whets the appetites of those new to mediation. For those experienced mediators who so far have not tried working as a co-mediator we hope it inspires them to give it a try. For students of mediation we trust it goes some way to answering the question 'what is co-mediation? For those who may find themselves in need of a mediator in the future we hope it gives some insight into the pros and cons of using a co-mediating partnership and for anyone who has just happened upon this book we hope it proves an interesting read.

Monica Hanaway
2011

Introduction

1. What do we mean by Psychologically Informed Mediation?

Monica Hanaway

What is Mediation?

There are many excellent books which detail the process of mediation but for readers who may not be familiar with the process, I shall give a brief overview.

Mediation is not new. History shows forms of mediation in use in Phoenician commerce, Ancient Greece and Rome. Many cultures have a 'wise elder' who may be seen as taking on an informal mediation role.

Today, mediation is regarded as a form of 'alternative dispute resolution' through which a neutral third party assists those in dispute to work towards their own settlement. It is used in a variety of disputes such as family, community, commercial, legal, diplomatic and workplace. It is fairly quick, in that many mediations take place in one day and are also much cheaper than legal alternatives. Unlike court proceedings it offers confidentiality, the only exceptions usually involve child abuse or actual or threatened criminal, violent or dangerous acts.

There are different styles of mediation including evaluative, facilitative and transformative. Evaluative mediators do evaluate the strengths and weaknesses of each side's argument should they go to court whereas facilitative mediators and transformative mediators are non-judgemental and so do not do this. All models share the advantage that they have the potential to come up with very creative solutions.

The goals of different mediation models also differ. Evaluative mediation has the main aim of settlement, while transformative mediation looks at conflict as a crisis in communication and seeks to help resolve the conflict, through enabling parties to develop a clearer understanding of their own beliefs, assumptions and needs, together with those of the person they are in conflict with. The agreements stemming from this approach are focused more on needs than wants, and importance is placed on safeguarding the self-esteem of all parties. It aims for a solution that is 'good enough,' with both parties feeling they have benefited from the process rather than one party feeling they have 'won' and the other 'lost'.

The structure of mediation can vary. Most start with a pre-mediation meeting or phone calls and the agreement of a pre-mediation contract covering ground rules such as confidentiality, who will attend, fees etc. In the Harvard model, (which I use), on the day of the mediation the mediator starts by seeing all parties together to reiterate the ground rules, the mediator's role, and how the day will work, before moving on to hear opening statements from all concerned. The parties will then adjourn to their own rooms and throughout the day the mediator will meet with each party separately and confidentially until there seems to be some common ground when the mediator will usually bring the parties together. Finally a written agreement is drawn up and signed by the parties and witnessed by the mediator.

In some models the parties never meet together, whilst in others they never separate.

The Harvard Model

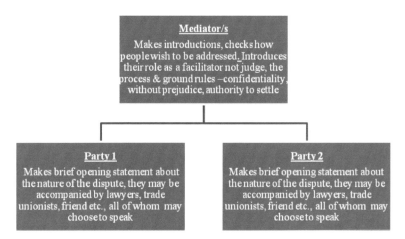

Fig 1.1 The opening – the mediator/s are in control of the process, not the content. Aim to make people feel comfortable and allow everyone to hear, perhaps for the first time, how each other sees things and how they feel about the dispute

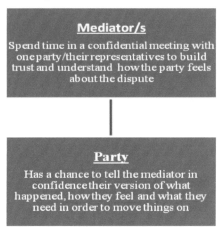

Fig 1.2 The Caucus – Each party has their own room to which the mediator will go for confidential meetings (caucus). The mediator aims to build a working alliance built on trust which will enable the party to tell them fully about the dispute

Having seen one party the mediator/s will go to the other party and repeat the process. This may happen several times until the mediator/s feels there is common ground which may benefit from bringing the parties back together.

Fig 1.3 At this stage the mediator/s seek to facilitate a dialogue between all involved and begins working to identify areas they can agree on to form a working document for the future (Heads of Agreement).

Things often arise during in this section which require further individual meetings and the process may be repeated many times before agreement is reached, written up, signed and witnessed.

There is much more to mediation than following a process. As we shall see, the key work of the mediator is to understand the parties in dispute, what is important to them and what might enable them to move on. The contributors to this book believe this to be necessary to acquire a real understanding of conflict and what it does to us psychologically.

What is conflict?

Before we explore the use of mediation and more specifically, co-mediation, in resolving conflict, it is important that we look briefly at what we understand by the term 'conflict' and indeed by what the authors understand by psychologically informed mediation. Not all mediators would see their work as being underpinned by a psychological understanding of inter relational human communication. However for the authors contributing here, their shared belief in mediation as a philosophical and psychological process lay at the heart of their decision to embark on this project.

Before we can mediate we must have a conflict which requires a resolution. So let us start by considering what we understand by 'conflict'. Most people asked to consider the word will come up with a set of negative emotions such as anger, aggression, fear, hostility or a similar set of nouns – fight, clash, argument etc.

Encarta defines conflict as,

> '*a continued struggle or battle, ... open warfare between opposing forces; disagreement or clash between ideas, principles, or people; a psychological state resulting from the often unconscious opposition between simultaneous but incompatible desires, needs, drives,*

or impulses; opposition between characters or forces in a literary work that shapes or motivates the action of the plot'

The nature of conflict has fascinated many thinkers from the start of time. There isn't space here to cover the different ways influential thinkers have written about conflict, suffice it to say that some (e.g. Aristotle) saw conflict as a negative human attribute which needed eliminating, whist others saw it as an essential component of change (e.g. Heraclitus, Hegel, Darwin).

By the time we come to the twentieth century, psychoanalysis saw a focus on inner and external conflicts whilst social scientists were taking a more sociological look at conflict. For writer such as Louis Coser (1913-2003), social conflict was caused by the struggle over limited resources. His main theme being, that conflict arises between an in group (us) and an out group (everyone else), and that it may be felt vital to neutralize or eliminate the rival group. Coser pointed out that conflict has a unifying function as it creates strong associations and cohesiveness within the respective groups, a theory which has been used in the creation of many team building programmes.

Following on from Coser, Morton Deutsch (1973) embraced conflict, seeing it as something which can be constructive. He posited that parties in a conflict may both be able to gain from the experience – it was not necessary that one side 'won' and the other 'lost' but that a 'win-win' outcome could occur.

Current approaches

The much derided Wikipedia offers us a 'political' definition within which, 'conflict' refers to an *'ongoing state of hostility between two groups of people'* and separates this from a definition of conflict resolution, which is given as, *"when two or more parties, with perceived incompatible goals, seek to undermine each other's goal-seeking capability"*. For me the sense of goals being 'perceived as incompatible' provides the mediator with a creative challenge – how to challenge these perceptions and move the parties in dispute from a place of 'stuckness' to a place of creative possibilities. In so doing mediators seek to find commonality, and most importantly, to move the parties from seeing the other as the enemy to identifying the dispute itself as a shared enemy, impacting negatively on them both.

Conflicts can be experienced as short term, shocking deviations within normally compatible and amicable relationships, or as deeply embedded long-term disagreements. This is reflected in the writings of a number of theorists who have looked at conflict.

Shantz (1987), defines conflicts as, *'time-distributed social episodes" consisting of a series of discrete components that include issues, oppositions, resolutions, and outcomes'*.

For Costintino and Merchant (1966), conflict is a fundamental disagreement between two parties, of which conciliation, conflict avoidance, capitulation or dispute are possible outcomes. They maintain that, *"a conflict can exist without a dispute, but a dispute cannot exist without a conflict."*

Douglas Yarn (1999) saw conflict as a state, rather than a process with people with opposing interests, values, or needs being in a state of conflict, which may be latent or manifest.

John Burton (1990) distinguishes between conflict and dispute by time and issues involved, suggesting short-term disputes are relatively easy to resolve whereas long-term conflicts may contain seemingly non-negotiable issues resistant to resolution. The main reason he holds this pessimistic view is that he identifies these long term conflicts as being focused on beliefs and value systems. Whenever such systems are challenged the individual's self-esteem is threatened and issues of self-worth, domination and rejection take precedent over more concrete material gains or losses. In other words the dispute takes on a very personal flavor and the psychological interplay and outcome is paramount.

It is this psychological approach with its emphasis on unearthing the value systems, emotional language and worldviews of the disputants and seeking to preserve or even enhance their self-esteem, through working with the fundamental human psychological needs for identity, security, and recognition, which Strasser and Randolph (2004) have developed in their approach to mediation. They see these elements as present in both disputes and conflicts.

'One of the most important elements of ... mediation ... is the exploration of the covert reasons for the dispute, as well as the overt. The parties will have developed rigid belief systems as their overall strategy for survival in an uncertain world...

Totton (2006), suggests that psychotherapeutic debate has focused on three questions around aggression –

'Is aggression an innate human trait, or is it the product of specific conditions? Is aggression wholly negative, or does it have positive aspects and expressions? Can therapy contribute either to minimizing aggression or to supporting its positive aspects?'

Whilst Freud (1930), believed aggression to be innate and dangerous,

'men are not gentle creatures who want to be loved ... they are, on the contrary, creatures among whose instinctual endowments are to be reckoned a powerful share of aggressiveness ... Homo homini lupus (man is a wolf to man). ... In consequence of this primary mutual hostility of human beings, civilized society is perpetually threatened with disintegration'

Reich (1967) disagreed, seeing human beings as essentially possessing *'natural decency, spontaneous honesty, mute and complete feelings of love'*, and seeing aggression as *'the life expression of the musculature, or the system of movement'*. Suttie (1936), built on Reich's work, claiming that hate and destructiveness were secondary reactions to threatened primal love and Melanie Klein based her theoretical approach on an innate conflict between love and hate which was dealt with by projecting our destructiveness into others and adopting the depressive position to address the task of reparation.

Conflicts are essential parts of our internal human nature. Samuels (1993) took a more political stance seeing aggression as lying at the heart of a pluralistic approach to politics, *'often masking the deepest need for contact, dialogue, playback, affirmation.'* Here we see a more positive approach to conflict, in which it is accepted as a precursor to growth and change, reflected in the work of scholars such as Mindell (1995) with his clarion cry of, *'Value trouble. Accept nature. Make peace with war'* and Totton's (2006) clarification of therapy's key contributions to this area,

> *'affirm aggression, support conflict, speak up for competition – while also affirming, supporting and speaking up for the victims of alienated and destructive expressions of these qualities.'*

How do we respond to conflict?

Conflicts occur when arguments, disagreements, competition or equalities threatens something which is important to us. This may be external– our job, family friendship, or internal – our self–esteem. It raises questions and thoughts such as –

I might lose my job

I'm losing control

I'm not being listened to

I'm not understood

I deserve respect

I'm losing control

I'm not being listened to

I'm not understood

I might be attacked

These are psychological responses to conflict which a mediator must understand. They may be accompanied by bodily reactions and expressed as fear, anger, loss of control, depression etc.

When we are faced with these kinds of questions we do not generally have a logical response. When we feel angry or threatened by a challenging conversation, situation or email we have what is termed 'an amygdala hijack', where our emotions take precedence over our actions. The emotional part of the brain, the amygdala, overrides the thinking part of the brain, the neocortex, in response to a perceived threat. This compromises the ability to reason and think logically. The working memory becomes less efficient and blood pressure, adrenaline and hormone levels rise. It can take 3 to 4 hours for it to clear the system.

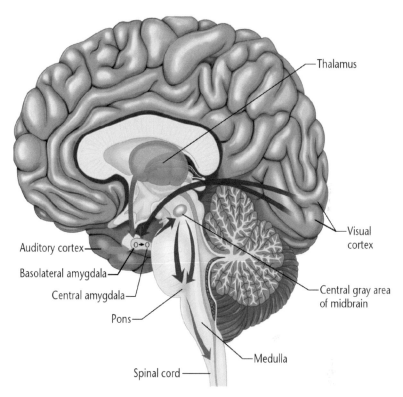

Fig 1.4 The brain's response to threat

People respond differently to the flood of hormones which occurs in an amygdala hijack. We prepare ourselves to deal with the perceived threat by either running away or standing our ground and fighting. For our cave-dwelling ancestors, this 'fight/flight response' was an essential tool for survival, evolved over many thousands of years living in wild and dangerous places where life or death threats from others, animals and the environment were ever present. Living in today's twenty-first century the response is still there but is often activated in situations where the threat is not of bodily extinction but may be felt as strongly.

The response starts when certain primitive parts of the brain send a message to the adrenal glands, which begin a process involving a number of hormones including adrenaline, whose purpose is to prepare the body for vigorous emergency action. Non-essential processes are immediately switched off. In particular, if the body is digesting food, that is stopped immediately, and people notice a feeling of churning or 'butterflies' in the stomach, or feeling nauseous or sick. A number of other changes follow, to make the muscles as strong as possible and eliminate from the body anything which is not needed or which may possibly slow you down.

The liver releases glucose into the bloodstream. Fats are released into the bloodstream from the fat stores in the body. These are fuel for the muscles, so oxygen is needed to burn them .The breathing increases, and may cause breathlessness. The body then needs to get fuel and oxygen to the muscles as soon as possible so the heart begins beating faster, sometimes causing palpitations. Blood pressure rises, and some people notice feeling hot or cold or begin sweating as the body seeks to dissipate the heat that will be generated by the vigorous muscular activity for which the body is preparing. Muscle tension increases, and a person may notice shaking, or becoming restless and chronic headaches or backache may result.

As all this is happening in the body, there are two important changes in the neurology. First, reflexes are speeded up. At the same time, so is the thinking process, and some people notice racing thoughts.

Second, the blood supply to the frontal parts of the brain which is responsible for higher levels of reasoning, is reduced, while the blood supply to the more primitive parts, near the brain stem, is increased. These parts are responsible for automatic, instinctive or impulsive decision making and behaviour. A stressed person may be prone to impulsive thinking and behaviour which they may regret later.

It is important that mediators understand what may be happening both psychologically and physiologically for the client. Yet, this is not enough. In order to work effectively with parties involved in conflict we must understand our own response to conflict –

Do I enjoy it?

Do I provoke it?

Do I fear it?

Do I go numb in the face of it?

Do I run from it?

Do I ignore it?

Do I tolerate it?

How does Psychologically Informed Mediation differ from other form of Mediation?

Some mediators do not consider these psychological functions when mediating a dispute. They are intent on solving the problem and finding a solution. For mediators taking a transformational approach, this psychological understanding lies at the heart of their work and governs their approach.

Psychologically informed mediators start with the belief that every individual is unique and intercommunication between individuals is innately complex, multi-dimensional and unpredictable. This is undeniably true in any conflict situation. Despite the fact that a dispute may seem relatively simple in the first instance, a mediator must ask, 'If that is the case why has it not resolved without my help?' It is rarely the surface issues which keep people in conflict, the more sedimented reasons, often hidden from the conscious awareness of the disputants, are often the cause of prolonged disagreement.

Kenneth Cloke (2006) believes,

> '*each person's attitudes, intentions, intuitions, awareness, context, and capacity for empathetic and honest emotional communication has a significant impact on their experience of conflict and capacity for resolution. As a result, no one can know objectively or in advance how to resolve any particular conflict, as anything chaotic and rapidly changing cannot be successfully predicted or managed.*'

My own training as an existential phenomenological psychotherapist influences my approach as a mediator. One of the existential shared givens is our need to be heard. This is a gift to a mediator. A common cause of conflict stems from a person not feeling listened to. The mediator has to aim to develop a trusting relationship with all involved in any mediation. It is this strong working alliance, with respectful and reflective listening at its heart, which can unlock the conflict.

Phenomenologists, drawing on the works of Edmund Husserl (1859-1938), base their understanding about how we exist in the world on the premise that objects exist through the meaning that we give. This is known as 'intentionality', which occurs unconsciously. Husserl saw every act of intentionality as containing two parts; 'noema' which is directional, '... *the object (the what) that we direct our attention towards and focus upon*' and 'noesis', which is referential, the 'how' through which we define an object.

It is important that we listen to both the noematic (content) and the noetic (the individual's unique emotional experience of that content). We can only begin to really understand when we listen for and to both aspects. Both these aspects are interpreted by the individual through the veils of their familial, cultural and individual experiences including their value sets and emotional context.

Mediation skills for psychologically informed mediation

There are a number of basic skills which help to elicit both these aspects. These include the use of encouraging body language, the use of silence, not interrupting, asking open questions, reflecting back, paraphrasing, summarising and the identification of themes which are tracked and deconstructed (rather than analysed). These allow the listener to feed back any contradictions between noema and noesis, between the values and actions, between the body language and verbal content or any other shifts in approach or outlook. They will explore the assumptions which are being expressed, and the emotional context of the statements. To do this effectively the mediator has to learn to set aside their own preconceptions and judgements and listen in an open way.

Using these skills, mediators develop greater understanding of the individual's response to the dispute (e.g. emotions, value and belief systems, coping strategies and factors influencing self-esteem) thus helping to understand their fundamental worldview, and facilitate a deeper and more authentic dialogue.

Emotions

If we listen to the noesis, then we are listening to emotions. People are never without emotions but the emotional context of what people say is often overlooked by the listener or disturbs the listener to such an extent that they attempt to filter it out. This may be due to lack of skill or fear of emotional expression. In understanding a person's emotional stance the mediator gains an entry to their psychological world and is helped to interact more effectively and empathically. Having one's own emotions noted may be a rare luxury which allows an individual to feel heard, leading to a major shift in the dispute, with an individual being more willing to move from a sedimented stance to a more fluid approach.

Values and Beliefs

By gaining insight into their emotional world we discover the centrality of an individual's value system. Emotions are always attached to something, whether the object is within the person's consciousness or not. We often feel at our most emotional if our beliefs or values are attacked in some way. The attack may come from others or ourselves (when we find ourselves behaving in ways which go against our beliefs).

By understanding this we can identify emotional stressors. A too rigid (or sedimented) adherence to a value may be problematic; for example, if an individual places 'loyalty' high in his/her value set they may feel the need to follow the behaviours of their peers or institution even when they experience those behaviours as destructive or wrong.

The task is not to challenge the values but to understand how they are being played out within the dispute, to challenge tensions, ambiguities or rigidity and to work towards a settlement which takes account of the values of the individual. To ignore these beliefs risks coming to a 'logical' solution in what is essentially an emotional situation.

Coping Strategies

People develop coping strategies in response to life's challenges. Often these work well and the individual automatically employs them without being conscious of doing so, they become an automatic response. A common strategy is to choose a position as a 'leader' or a 'follower'. For some their successful coping strategy is to adopt a leadership position and to forge forward, hopefully taking others with them. Others may adopt a position as follower preferring not to be in the front line. It does not mean that by taking a follower position one cannot lead. Many good leaders seek out the opinions of others, empower others and lead from the back.

Unfortunately a coping strategy which works well in most circumstances can cause problems in others. In a mediation the disputant can see different ways of coping without losing self-esteem.

Through the mediation process, the mediator has to be both follower and a leader. The mediator has to 'tune in' to the unique world of the individuals and to follow their stories without any judgement. The mediator follows where the party takes them, respecting and working with the values, emotions and coping strategies expressed, in order to explore their perception of the dispute.

Challenging

People in conflict often feel powerless. It is important that disputants are reminded of their responsibilities and potential for choice. Although we are unable to change the incident which led to the dispute, we can change our attitude towards it.

Tuning in is not enough. The disputant has to learn to understand and be sensitive to the perceptions of the other without getting stuck in their newly found mutuality and ignoring what steps need to be taken to address the specific conflict and move towards a resolution. This can only occur when trust has been established and both parties are respectfully heard. People are more inclined to be open and creative if they feel they have been listened to with respect. They no longer have to fight their corner because there is no one to fight against – the have been heard and witnessed. Identifying when that moment has arrived is a skill which uses knowledge of human behaviour but also relies heavily on experience.

The mediator may help the individuals identify what might happen if they choose not to agree to a resolution (e.g. go to court, lose their job, their family, their pride, their self-esteem etc.). It is equally creative and sometimes surprising to consider what would happen if they do get exactly what was asked for, as there may well be losses attached. Getting what they thought they wanted may achieve material gain but fail to bring the emotional state they were hoping for.

Self-esteem

People in conflict often have low self-esteem stemming from a sense of embarrassment that they have been unable to resolve the dispute. They may feel disempowered and have lost any sense that they have the power to choose how they respond to the dispute.

To maintain a good level of self-esteem we need opportunities for self-expression and respectful listening. We need to understand the worldviews and responses to conflict of the disputants– do they provoke it, fear it, enjoy it, tolerate it, run from it or see it as an opportunity for creativity? The mediator works with the disputant to help clarify his or her own stance.

A psychologically informed mediator will seek to maintain or even increase the self-esteem of all those involved in the mediation. At the same time they will haul in their own natural desire to increase their own self esteem by appearing to know the answers and to hold the solution in their hands. The disputants are always responsible for the solution the mediator's role is one of facilitation and so holds the responsibility for the process but not for the content.

The psychological ebb and flow within the mediation process

Unfortunately, the mediation process is neither chronological nor linear. The trusting working alliance may be built and lost a number of times throughout the process. The 'tuning in' process (through active listening), is the central element in building that alliance, with the requirement to enter into the other's worldview, with its value sets, coping strategies and emotional reactions.

Once the alliance is established and an understanding of the other's worldview developed, the parties in the dispute need to 'tune out' and enter back into the 'world of the dispute' with its concrete and emotional implications. By moving into this phase we begin to focus on possible solutions in order to facilitate a 'good enough' solution.

When mediating I hold an internal image of a funnel with the early parts of the process being very open – the mediator following the party, whereas towards the end of the process the focus needs to be narrowed down, becoming more focused towards identifying potential areas of commonality amongst the parties the dispute and grounds for potential agreement.

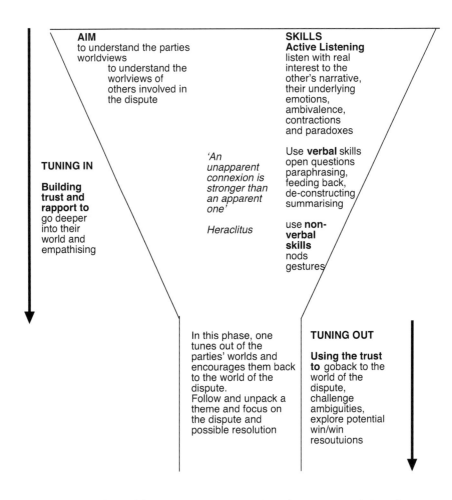

Fig 1.5: Funnel model: Hanaway (2008) – To show 'tuning in' and tuning out' stages of mediation.

In 'tuning in' the emphasis lies in consciously listening for descriptors of the inner world of the speaker showing their values, emotions and behaviour patterns. It is important to take everything which is said as being of equal importance and significance. Heraclitus found every 'unapparent' connection to be stronger than an 'apparent' one. Freud and other psychoanalysts taught us to accept that all that is presented contains unconscious communications as well as conscious ones. The client may find it hard to tell the mediator things which make him/her feel vulnerable, silly, or guilty, or where they feel the mediator may potentially disagree with them. They may experience paradoxical responses to the dispute and/or the people involved.

The mediator may pick up on any theme, even if it seems very far removed from the actual dispute, and unpack it, controlling their own needs to offer a solution or make 'inspirational' links. At this stage the client is the leader, and the mediator follows, slowly unwrapping the meaning of what is being presented through paraphrasing, reflecting back and summarizing without judgement. The mediator trusts in the process and believes that everything told to them in the early part of the process will be relevant, giving indicators of the values, life strategies and emotional stance of the speaker.

This intense listening in itself builds trust which can then be used to focus down/tune out, allowing the focus to become firmly on the conflict and its possible resolutions. The mediator can then challenge the client to think differently about their response to the dispute and to consider what they really want as an outcome.

Conclusion

The authors believe that, whether working as a sole mediator, or as a co-mediator, it is essential to have an understanding of some of the psychological factors which are in play when people are in conflict. Whilst at the same time it is important to start with the belief in the uniqueness of individual experience.

The psychologically informed mediator puts energy into developing a trusting working alliance with each individual disputant through listening and seeking to understand their unique stance on the dispute. Unlike some mediators they will not try to rush the parties into a resolution. The process is valued as much as the agreement. It is hoped that the process will not just result in the solution to one point of dispute but may result in the disputants having a greater understanding of themselves, helping to prevent further conflict.

If working with another mediator it is essential that both mediators share the same philosophy as to the meaning and place of conflict and the role of the mediator in helping to facilitate a resolution.

<u>References</u>

Burgess, Heidi and Brad Spangler. "Conflicts and Disputes." *Beyond Intractability*. Eds. Guy Burgess and Heidi Burgess. Conflict Research Consortium, University of Colorado, Boulder.
Posted: July 2003   http://www.beyondintractability.org/essay/conflicts_disputes/.

Burton, J. 1990. '*Conflict: Resolution and Prevention*'. London: St Martin's Press.

Cloke K., (2006), *The Crossroads of Conflict: A Journey into the Heart of Dispute Resolution,* Janis Publications

Costintino, C.A. and Merchant C.S. *Designing Conflict Management Systems: A Guide to Creating Productive and Healthy Organizations*. San Francisco: Jossey-Bass, 1996, pp 4-5

Craig Y.J., (1998), '*Advocacy, Counselling and Mediation in Casework*',
London: Jessica Kingsley Publishers

Deutch M., (1973), 'The Resolution of Conflict', Yale University Press

Freud S., (1930) *'Civilisation and Its Discontents'*, Penguin Freud Library , London: Penguin 1985

Glasl F., (1999), 'Confronting Conflict', Bristol: Hawthorn Press

Hicks. T., (1996-2000), Seven steps for effective problem-solving in the workplacehttp//www.conflict-resolution.net/articles/index.cfm edn.

Jensen-Campbell, L. A., Graziano, W. G., & Hair, E. C. (1996), *'Personality and relationships as moderators of interpersonal conflict in adolescence'*. Merrill-Palmer Quarterly, 42, 148–164.

Kovel J., (1995). On Racism and Psychoanalysis, in Elliot A. & Frosch S. (eds),
'Psychoanalysis in Contexts' London: Routledge

Liebmann M (ed.)., (2000), *'Mediation in Context'*, London: Jessica Kingsley Publishers

Mindell A., (1995) *'Sitting in the fire: Large group Transformation Using Conflict and Diversity'*, San Francisco; Harper Collins'

Reich W., (1967), *'Reich speaks of Freud'*, London:Condor

Samuels A., (1993), *'The Political Psyche'*, London: Routledge

Shantz, C. U. (1987), Conflicts between students. *Child Development, 58, pp.*283-305

Scheff T, Retzinger S.' *Emotions* and *Violence'*. Lexington, MA: Lexington Books; 1991.

Strasser F. & Randolph P., (2004), *'Mediation – A Psychological Insight into Conflict Resolution'*, London: Continuum.

Suttie I., (1936), *'The Origins of Love and Hate'* Harmondsworth: Penguin

Tantam D. (2002), *'Psychotherapy and Counselling in Practice – a narrative Framework'*, Cambridge: Cambridge University Press

Totton N., (2006), *'The Politics of Psychotherapy"*, Maidenhead: Open University Press

Vuchinich, S. (1990). 'The sequential organization of closing in verbal family conflict'. In A. D. Grimshaw (Ed.), *'Conflict talk: Sociolinguistic investigations of arguments in conversations'* (pp. 118–138). New York: Cambridge Univ. Press.

Yarn, D. H. ed. "Conflict" in *Dictionary of Conflict Resolution*, San Francisco: Jossey-Bass 1999. p. 115.

2. The History of Co-Mediation

Tricia Hayes

Introduction

To talk about the history of co-mediation is to talk about the history of mediation itself as a form of third party intervention in dispute resolution. Mediation, from the Latin *'mediare'* or *'place in the middle'* (Compact Oxford English Dictionary, 2000) has become widely recognised as an alternative dispute resolution (ADR) method and has been defined as *'a process by which an impartial third party helps two (or more) disputants work out how to resolve a conflict. The disputants, not the mediators, decide the terms of any agreement reached. Mediation usually focuses on future rather than past behaviour'* (Liebmann, 2000:10). Despite relatively common definitions, however, rigorous debate continues as to the constitution of mediation practice, the attributes of the mediators and so on, with little real consensus between the various perspectives.

This chapter explores how, in the study and practice of the mediation method in Western society, co-mediation has emerged as a strategy rather than a defining feature of the mediation method. It also explores this emergence within the context of traditional approaches to dispute resolution including third party involvement and looks at the implications for the future development of the mediation method. The chapter starts with a brief history on mediation and its revival in 1950's USA, particularly the growth of community mediation services. It then looks at how the literature presents co-mediation and how this relates to third party involvement generally, cross culturally and more specifically in Western society dispute resolution. The focus then turns to the development of mediation in the USA and the dominance of a particular vision in the practice and study of mediation concluding with a discussion of the implications for the continued practice and study of co-mediation.

History of Mediation and its 20th Century Revival

Mediation as a feature of human behaviour has existed from the fifth century B.C. particularly, but not only, in China, Japan and Korea (Kim et al, 1993; Yarn, 2000; Honeyman et al, 2004). It is seen as a product of the evolution of various approaches to conflict resolution (Pinzon, 1996) and has been supported and encouraged by rulers and delivered by specific trusted individuals, elders or even whole communities coming together to manage conflict situations (Kim et al, 1993; Fry, 2000; Meyer, 2002). The formal practice of mediation as a dispute resolution method dates from the early nineteenth century with evidence of it being used in international conflicts (Strasser & Randolph, 2004).

The revival of mediation in the United States in the 1950's, particularly community mediation was informed by 'popular justice' practices prevalent in Cuba, the Soviet Union and China (Merry & Milner, 1993). Popular justice refers to dispute resolution processes that serve as alternatives to state law, where procedures are informal and disputants reach agreement consensually with the aid of a third party removed from the dispute. Merry & Milner (1993:4-10) characterise popular justice as being '*on the boundary between state law and local or community ordering*' and argue that '*community mediation hoped to replace the dominance of the legal profession and the courts in the lives of ordinary citizens with the control of neighbours and peers*'. Merry (1993:40) describes four different forms of popular justice; '*reformist, socialist, communitarian and anarchic*', all of which have '*a distinct vision the contribution popular justice will make to the social and political transformation of society*'.

Reformist and socialist traditions are more closely allied to state law and government regulation where communitarian and anarchic traditions are concerned with self-regulation and are viewed by proponents as the antithesis of state law (Merry, 1993). These differing visions of dispute resolution manifest in the conflict resolution literature in different ways, for example, Bush (1996:735) talks about *'top-down organising'* (directive intervention) versus *'bottom-up self-initiation'* (non-directive intervention), where top-down intervention concerns the imposition of outcomes to resolve disputes and bottom-up intervention concerns the resolution of disputes by means of consensus and reconciliation. They are also evident in Yarn's (2000:58) discussion of dispute resolution within the context of human and non-human primate dispute intervention paradigms that are, essentially, based on patterns of behaviour around *'dominance and submission'* (equating to directive intervention) and *'co-operation and altruism'* (equating to non-directive intervention).

Benjamin (1990) discusses them within the context of scientific thinking and the shift from Newtonian physics to quantum mechanics and the theory of relativity i.e., the move from traditional prescriptive, rational, technical approaches to dispute resolution to more interactive, dynamic and intuitive approaches. Wehr & Lederach (1991) present them in terms of differing theoretical concepts of mediation, firstly the neutrality-based model where the mediators are anonymous and relate to the disputants only in terms of their role in managing the conflict and secondly the trust-based model where the mediators are closely connected to the disputants and have a trusted relationship with them which continues when the dispute ends. Each of these authors in their own way highlight the competing forces that operate individually and collectively in the face of conflict i.e., movement towards retribution or movement towards reconciliation.

Mediation services, particularly community services, mushroomed in the United States in the 1950's and formalising mediation as an alternative dispute resolution method began from the 1970's when it became evident that traditional dispute resolution methods, particularly litigation, were yielding unsatisfactory outcomes (Coy & Hedeen, 2005). The idea that dispute resolution could be less time consuming, less costly and less emotionally draining was argued to be one of the most attractive incentives behind the revival of mediation, other ideas concerned social change aspirations and the development of personal conflict management skills (Harrington & Merry, 1988).

Mediation was already in use to resolve labour disputes through the Federal Mediation and Conciliation Service (FMCS) and by early 1953; seminal work was done by labour dispute mediators in describing the role and practices of the mediator (Birke & Titz, 1991; Barrett, 1999). With the growing popularity of mediation, the American Arbitration Association began developing guidelines and training for its application and institutions such as the Society of Professionals in Dispute Resolution (SPIDR) and the National Institution of Dispute Resolution (NIDR) were instrumental in developing performance and assessment standards (Folberg & Taylor, 1984; Harrington & Merry, 1988; Milner, 1996).

By the late 1980's, according to Harrington & Merry (1988:712), approximately 350 community mediation services were in operation across the United States and they suggest that while many of these services were court-based,

> *'there has also been a proliferation of religious-based, social-service based, and community-based programs"*
> *also that "the field of community mediation is diverse and somewhat untamed, not all programs follow the judicial mode'. Lederach & Kraybill (1993:371)*

provide an interesting contrast between the differing mediation contexts "at one extreme are the neighbourhood centres espousing volunteerism, self-help and peer relationships. At the other end are highly trained professionals who want to make a decent livelihood carving out a niche in the professional world of help somewhere between career diplomats, organisational consultants, lawyers and therapists".

One of the interesting aspects in the application of the mediation method within the different contexts was that, arguably, historic patterns were repeated in terms of the number of mediators delivering the method, for example, in the top-down approach, the tendency seemed towards a solo practitioner approach while in the bottom-up approach the tendency seemed towards a team approach (Folberg & Taylor, 1984; Merry & Milner, 1993; Beer & Steif, 1997). This was an interesting development in that both approaches applied an automatic interpretation of the constitution of the third party, however, given Folberg & Taylor's (1984:144) assertion that *'two mediators may double the cost of the service'*, then the significance of justifying the use of two mediators becomes somewhat clearer.

The differing interpretations of the constitution of the third party have not received any real attention in the literature despite their application in practice, although the differing mediation contexts themselves continue to serve as the basis for much debate on the meaning and purpose of the mediation method. The questions raised by Menkel-Meadow (1995:219) remain as pertinent now as they were when they were raised *'who 'owns' the conflict ... is reduction or 'management' of the conflict the goal or is the mediation process designed to accomplish other social goals'?* These questions are considered by Mayer (2004:151) in terms of mediation being regarded either as a social movement or a profession. He argues that the danger of professionalization is the risk that mediation will be absorbed completely by other professional disciplines particularly (but not only) law and of being a social movement that,

> *'our belief in the larger impact of our work can encourage us to overlook the immediate needs of our*

clients or the people involved in the conflicts we are working on'.

In any case, subscribing to one view has implications which Pinzon (1996:16) describes in terms of accepting

'systems of power that are producing a particular 'truth', systems of power with deep and specific economic, social and political consequences; and a dynamics of power that will try, through the generation of new 'rational' discourses, to maintain the structure and legitimacy of this truth'.

The mediation literature abounds with research on what constitutes the mediation process (Kressel, 2000; Bush & Folger, 2005; Alexander, 2008) what mediators do (Bercovitch & Houston, 2000; Jacobs & Aakhus, 2002); mediator knowledge and skills (Herrman et al, 2001 & 2002), down to the type of people mediators are likely to be *'victims or children of the holocaust, of alcoholics, of divorce, of diasporas'* (Menkel-Meadow,1995:222); *'folkloric trickster figures'* (Benjamin, 2003:87). What continues to be glaringly absent from the literature, however, is a focus on the significance of the actual constitution of the third party i.e., the number of mediators who deliver the method.

There is some recognition of this gap, for example, Kaufman & Duncan (1992:703) acknowledge

'... we do not address situations with two mediators (common in small claims, community and school peer mediation) or with mediation teams (as in international mediation) as they are complicated by the relations among the mediators and their possible divergent views on strategy ... the interaction of mediators is a fertile research field that is little explored'.

Other research again simply makes reference to the value of

a team approach without any real insight on its potential, for example, Bercovitch & Houston (2000) acknowledge that the number of mediators involved in the delivery of a mediation session does have some influence, although the study is not concerned with examining what that influence is; Menkel-Meadow (1993:375) also makes reference to mediating teams as in *'students working in teams mediated general civil cases of all types'* but without any explanation on the significance of the team arrangement. Any attention given to co-mediation tends to be limited to the contribution it makes towards achieving settlement, rather than on the co-mediation dynamic itself and consequently co-mediation is not a well-defined concept in the literature.

The 1982 practice model of the Friends Conflict Resolution Programme is arguably one of the first to introduce and advocate for the arrangement of a team approach to mediation practice, which is described as a strategy to enhance delivery of the mediation method (Beer & Steif, 1997). It highlights the 'process' benefits of co-mediation for both the mediators and the disputants such as division of tasks, skills development, self-evaluation and modelling collaboration.

Co-mediation as a strategy is also validated by Folberg & Taylor (1984:140) on the basis that,

> *'individual mediators rarely have the interdisciplinary training, experience or expertise to address fully the combined emotional, legal, and technical aspects present in some cases'.*

They proceed to identify a number of advantages, both process and outcome related, such as gender balancing, subject/process expertise and peer training. However, they also caution against the use of co-mediation arguing that for every advantage there is a corresponding disadvantage, adding that *'the resources involved in co-mediation are greater and represent an added cost, regardless of how it is paid or absorbed'* (p144).

This is an interesting assertion when considered within the context of the development of community mediation services with communitarian rather than socialist visions of dispute resolution. In this context, the number of mediators and cost is meaningless since mediation is about non-professional, self-governing groups of people working together to resolve disputes. This vision of dispute resolution resonates with the peace-keeping traditions among Quaker and Mennonite religions (Wehr & Lederach, 1991; Beer & Steif, 1997); Native American Indian justice systems (Meyer, 2002) also peace-keeping traditions in non-Western egalitarian societies, for example, Morrill & McKee (1993:447) suggest that,

'anthropologists had long studied indigenous moots in which groups of villagers gathered to facilitate discussion among disputants, to provide therapy via group discussion for victims and offenders, and to reintegrate the principals into local communities".

Efforts to recreate this vision of mediation are evident from the growth of non-court based community mediation services in the USA such as the influential San Franciso Community Boards whose goals are described as *'neighbourhood building ... developing a neighbourhoods capacity to respond to neighbourhood disputes'* (Fitzpatrick, 1993:456). This vision of mediation as a group or a combined effort contrasts greatly with the vision of mediation as a discrete process applied by a specialist, yet it is the latter that receives the bulk of attention in the mediation literature, limiting the practice of co-mediation to situations that merit its use.

Guidelines on the use of co-mediation are presented by Love & Stulberg (1996:188) who conclude that: *'...many trainers, academics, program administrators and rule-makers are calling for co-mediation in a variety of contexts and for a variety of purposes...'* Love & Stulberg's conclusion is further borne out in the literature with more recent support for the justification of co-mediation in terms of subject/process expertise (Susskind

2000; Wall 2001); mediator health and safety (Mulcahy & Summerfield, 2001); gender dynamics (Picard 2002); mentoring and professional development (Lang & Taylor, 2000; Bowling & Hoffman, 2003); ethnic connectedness (Honeyman, 2004). Research carried out in Ireland among mediation trainers revealed that, apart from community mediation where co-mediation is the norm both in training and practice, the views expressed correspond with those expressed in the literature i.e., its value as a strategy to enhance delivery of the process (Hayes, 2006).

It is clear from the above that there are different visions behind the revival of 20th century mediation, visions that are played out in the mediation literature and in mediation practice (Merry & Milner, 1993; Bush & Folger, 2005). It is also clear that the prevailing vision of mediation, currently held by theorists and practitioners alike, is one where the practice of co-mediation is only recognised in terms of what additional knowledge a second mediator can bring, be it in relation to the substantive content or contextual aspects of the dispute. However, with the continuing increase in the variety of contexts and purposes where co-mediation is used, particularly the replication of certain disputant characteristics in the co-mediating team (Honeyman et al, 2004), the eventual justification for its use in every context and for every purpose is, arguably, inevitable.

Two Mediate or Not Two Mediate

Given the increased attention in the literature for the justification of co-mediation, the obvious question then becomes, when is it ever un-justified? To further understand how co-mediation has evolved in Western society as a strategy rather than a defining feature of the mediation method requires an examination of third party involvement generally in dispute resolution. Anthropology scholars point to the significance of cultural traditions in understanding third party involvement in dispute resolution, for example, Harrington & Merry (1988:731) argue that,

> '*the way societies handle disputes is culturally constructed, and the meaning of the disputes and of resolution varies greatly from one cultural framework to another*'.

Fry (2000:336) examines patterns in dispute resolution across a variety of cultures and suggests that in certain societies where mediation is practiced, multiple mediators is the norm

> '*...several elders typically mediate disputes among East Indians of Fiji ... the Dou Donggo, the Limbus of Nepal .. Court ordered mediation sessions lead by trained volunteers in Finland...*'

He concludes that '*the use of particular third party settlement agents relates in part to the degree of authoritativeness inherent in specific types of social organisation*'.

Aureli & De Waal (2000:262) further argue that

> '*the study of impartial interventions as devices for conflict management needs therefore to consider the general features of social organisation as much as the acts of the single individuals*'

while Morill & McKee, 2005:460) argue that

> '*more broad ranging cross-sectional and longitudinal studies of the organisational fields of social control processes ... may provide a more complete understanding of the organisational processes of social control in modern society*".

So while the literature acknowledges that the choice to have solo or multiple mediators varies across societies, there is also recognition that the rationale behind such choices needs to be explored in greater depth.

A widely accepted feature of traditional third party involvement in dispute resolution in Western society, particularly in top-down approaches, is that the third party is a solo intervener who is removed from the dispute, with no allegiance or connection to the disputants, holding a neutral position that allows objective settlement or resolution of the dispute (Wehr & Lederach, 1991; Benjamin, 2003).   The role the third party takes depends mainly upon whether the process is a state or non-state process, for example, where state or legal processes are concerned the third party may weighs up evidence and have the authority to impose a solution to settle the dispute.   In non-state or conciliatory processes, the third party is more concerned with reconciling and resolving differences between the disputants and lacks any authority to impose a solution, relying instead on the co-operation of the disputants to reach consensus (Yarn, 2000). Tensions between state and non-state processes according to Folger & Bush (1994:5) relate to *'procedural formalities'* that serve to regulate third party influence in state processes and the absence of these formalities in mediation are perceived as posing a risk for disputants who are vulnerable to third party *'dispositions, preferences and prejudices'*.   In defending the informal nature of mediation, Folger & Bush (1994:4) argue that, in reality, the interventions of third parties in state and non-state processes follow similar patterns and suggest,

> *'third parties may be as responsive to characteristics of the dispute, disputants, and unfolding interaction as they are to the formal intervention mandates they bring to the process'.*

Nonetheless, it is clear from the literature that the development of mediation has been strongly shaped by practices related to state processes that reflect particular Western ideologies on dispute resolution.

According to Bush & Folger (2005:244-259) conflicting Western ideologies on dispute resolution fall into two categories of *'the ideology of social separation and conflict control'* and the *'ideology of social connection and conflict transformation'* which essentially represent different beliefs about human nature and dispute resolution, the latter that conflict is an opportunity for growth, the former that conflict leads to negative interaction. These ideologies have manifested in the mediation field as the problem-solving or settlement oriented approach to practice, often referred to as the individualist and relational approaches respectively. The settlement-oriented approach corresponds with the view of mediation as a problem-solving process that is economical, efficient and yields satisfaction and, according to Bush (1996:728), seeks to,

> *'exert pressure on parties to define disputes in terms of tangible issues, to agree on concrete measures to address these issues, and to conform their agreements to the mediator's own views of fairness, optimality etc.".* The transformative approach corresponds with the view of mediation as a process of developing "individual empowerment and empathy for others" (Milner, 1996:739)

and seeks to

> *'turn conflict interaction away from alienation from both self and other, toward a renewed connection to both, restoring strength of self and understanding of other, even while conflict continues' (Bush & Folger, 2005:78).*

The settlement-oriented approach has been widely accepted as being the predominant approach within the mediation field and consequently much of the debate in the literature is on its characteristics, assessment and validation as the essence of mediation (Folger & Bush, 1994; Pinzon, 1996; Mayer, 2004; Bush & Folger, 2005). Interestingly, co-mediation is not attributed specifically to either perspective, which is not surprising when arguably two mediators, in the same way as one mediator, can easily be (consciously or unconsciously) oriented towards the settlement or transformative perspective, for example, in the study by Jacobs & Aakhus (2002:182) where both mediators seemed to be '...*pressing for proposals to solve the problem rather than encouraging further argument to resolve differences in the two accounts or to reconcile differences of opinion*'. Any attention to co-mediation is typically within the context of settlement-oriented practices highlighting its benefits as a strategy to compensate for perceived deficits in the process or substantive expertise of solo mediators.

More recent research highlights the benefits in matching disputant characteristics, for example, in the study by Honeyman et al (2004:490) they suggest that the success of the mediation was essentially due to the disputants identifying, ethnically, with one of the mediators. They argue that the *'trappings of community connection and local authority'* together with expected *'competence, ethics and dedication'* makes for a winning formula in a mediation team and that such a combination instils confidence and trust in the method. The suggestion here is that the more the mediator(s) share the characteristics of the disputants they are working with the more likely the outcome will be productive. Wehr & Lederach (1991:87) also argue that mediator connection and closeness (insider-partials) can be equally as effective in dispute resolution as mediator anonymity (outsider-neutrals). They suggest that while credibility and legitimacy are linked to mediator anonymity, neutrality and professional credentials, a feature of North American mediation practices, the opposite is true for Central America where mediator partiality and connectedness give credibility and legitimacy, on the basis of trusted relationships that will continue when the dispute is ended. Kydd (2006:459) also suggests that *'mediation works best when the parties and the mediator share some bonds and are part of a recognisable network of interdependence'*.

The conceptualisation of mediation as presented by Wehr & Lederach (1991) represents a move towards the vision of dispute resolution within communitarian traditions, of collective deliberation, as practiced to some extent in Western community mediation services (Merry & Milner, 1993), however, as Morrill & McKee (1993:450) argue,

'the increasing stress on professionalization, and the detachment of mediators from the communities they serve suggest that community mediation organizations will become even more isomorphic with established state social control organizations in the future'.

This has implications for the continued practice of co-mediation as a natural arrangement within community mediation services and consequently for its study and research in terms of the interactions of the mediators and their orientation towards settlement-oriented and transformative approaches to practice.

Conclusion

The evidence from the literature suggests that there is an organic and mechanistic dimension to mediation. Organic in the sense that conflict can be managed through peaceful interaction (bottom-up) and mechanistic in the sense that systems are there to ensure that conflict is managed in particular ways (top-down). Both of these dimensions operate on an underlying principle of third party involvement that is interpreted differently by both in practice, specifically the number of mediators constituting the third party. Theory and research assume the mediator as a solo intervener, a specialist or an expert creating the conditions and environment, including the participation of a second mediator when necessary, to enable settlement of the dispute (Folberg & Taylor, 1984; Love & Stulberg, 1996). The extent of the potential that co-mediation offers cannot be fully appreciated until theory and research pays sufficient attention to it as a defining feature of mediation. One of perceived functions of mediation is that it leads to positive interaction (Gold, 2003; Honeyman et al, 2004) and the psychology literature would argue that one way to effect positive interaction as a behaviour is to model that behaviour. The significance of modelling desired behaviour as a technique in effecting behaviour change is well documented in psychology literature (Bandura, 1977; Mischel, 1993). While Folberg & Taylor (1984) do make reference to the potential of modelling positive interaction, research has paid little attention to mediator interactions and their effects (Kauffman & Duncan, 1992).

In order to realistically characterise the profession, theory, research and mediator training programmes need to focus on the true potential of co-mediation in terms of understanding its validity as a defining characteristic of the mediation method. Lowering risk of mediator bias, modelling positive interaction and exploring human interconnections are just three areas of potential that at the moment seem to be completed ignored. Since there is clearly awareness in the literature of the true potential co-mediation holds, focusing on it in terms of recognising and promoting it as a defining characteristic of the mediation method can also become a reality. However, while the current pattern seems to be that discovery of its potential is dependent upon the practice being applied (out of necessity) and most training programmes are still not including co-mediation skills/dynamics, then it could be argued that the characterisation of mediation as an ADR method will never be truly realised. Within the broader context of the development of mediation as a profession, it could be argued that to continually ignore the potential significance of the number of mediators conducting mediations is to deny mediation the opportunity of a fair assessment or evaluation and more importantly to impede the discovery of its true value as an ADR method.

References

Alexander N. (2008), The Mediation Metamodel: Understanding Practice. *Conflict Resolution Quarterly,* 26(1), p97-123

Aureli F. & De Waal F.B.M. (2000) *Natural Conflict Resolution,* California: University of California Press

Bandura A. (1977) *Social Learning Theory* New York: General Learning Press

Barrett J.T. (1999) In Search of the Rosetta Stone of the Mediation Profession. *Negotiation Journal* 15(3), p219-227

Baruch Bush, R.A. & Folger, J.P. (2005) *The Promise of Mediation, The Transformative Approach to Conflict, Revised Edition',* San Francisco: Jossey-Bass

Beer J.E. & Steif E. (1997) *The Mediator's Handbook (3rd Edition)* Philadelphia

Benjamin R. (1990) The Physics of Mediation: Reflections of Scientific Theory in Professional Mediation Practice. *Mediation Quarterly,* 8(2), p91-113

Benjamin, R. (2003) *Mediators, Tricksters and the Constructive Uses of Deception* in Bowling, D. & Hoffman, D. (2003), *Bringing Peace into the Room: How the Personal Qualities of the Mediator Impact the Process of Conflict Resolution* San Francisco: Jossey-Bass

Bercovitch, J. & Houston, A. (2000) Why Do They Do It Like This? *The Journal of Conflict Resolution,* 44(2), p170-202

Birke, R. & Teitz, L.E. (2002) U.S. Mediation in 2001: The Path the Brought America to Uniform Laws and Mediation in Cyberspace. *The American Journal of Comparative Law,* 50, (Supplement) p181-213

Bowling, D. & Hoffman, D. (2003) *Bringing Peace into the Room How the Personal Qualities of the Mediator Impact the Process of Conflict Resolution* San Franciso: Jossey-Bass

Bush, R.A.B. (1996) The Unexplored Possibilities of Mediation: A Comment on Merry and Milner. *Law and Social Inquiry,* 21(30, p715-736)

Compact English Dictionary (2000) London: Oxford University Press

Coy P.G. & Hedeen T. (2005) A Stage Model of Social Movement Co-optation: Community Mediation in the United States. *The Sociological Quarterly,* 46(3), p.405-435

Folberg J. & Taylor A. (1984) *A Comprehensive Guide to Resolving Conflicts without Litigation* San Francisco: Jossey-Bass

Folger J.P. & Bush R.A.B. (1994) in Folger J.P. & Jones T. (1994) *New Directions in Mediation, Communication Research and Perspectives* California: Sage Publications Inc.

Fry D. H. (2000) Law, Love, and Reconciliation: Searching for Natural Conflict Resolution in Homo sapiens. In Aureli, F. & De Waal, F.B.M. (2000) *Natural Conflict Resolution,* California: University of California Press

Gold L. (2003) *Mediation and the Culture of Healing* In Bowling, D. & Hoffman, D. (2003) *Bringing Peace into the Room How the Personal Qualities of the Mediator Impact the Process of Conflict Resolution* San Franciso: Jossey-Bass

Harrington C.B. & Merry S.E. (1988) Ideological Production the Making of Community Mediation *Law & Society Review* 12(4), p709-736

Hayes P.B. (2006) Two Mediate or Not Two Mediate: The Definition and Value of Co-Mediation in Ireland. *Unpublished*

Herrman M.S., Hollett, N., Gale, J. & Foster, M. (2001) Defining Mediator Knowledge and Skills *Negotiation Journal,* 17(2), p139-153

Herrman M.S., Hollett N., Eaker D.G., Gale J. & Foster M. (2002) Supporting Accountability in the Field of Mediation. *Negotiation Journal,* 18(1), p29-49

Honeyman C. Goh B.C. & Kelly L. (2004) Seeking Connectedness and Authority in Mediation *Negotiation Journal,* 20(4), p489-511

Jacobs S. & Aakhus M. (2002) What Mediators Do with Words: Implementing Three Models of Rational Discussion in Dispute Mediation. *Conflict Resolution Quarterly,* 20(2), p177-203

Kim N.H., Wall Jnr J.A., Sohn D.W. & Kim J.S. (1993) Community and Industrial Mediation in South Korea *Conflict Resolution Quarterly,* 37(2), p361-381

Kaufman S. & Duncan, G.T. (1992), A Formal Framework for Mediator Mechanisms and Motivations. *Journal of Conflict Resolution,* 36(4), p688-708

Kressel, K. (2000), In Deutsch, M. & Coleman, P.T. *The Handbook of Conflict Resolution, Theory and Practice* San Francisco: Jossey-Bass

Kydd, A.H. (2006), When Can Mediators Build Trust. *The American Political Science Review,* 100(3), p449-462

Lang M.D. & Taylor A. (2000) *The Making of a Mediator Developing Artistry in Practice* San Franciso: Jossey-Bass

Lererach J.P. & Kraybill, B. (1993) The Paradox of Popular Justice: A Practitioner's View. In Merry, S. & Milner, N. (1993) *The Possibility of Popular Justice: A Case Study of Community Mediation in the United States.* USA: The

University of Michigan Press

Liebmann M. (2000) *Mediation in Context* London: Jessica Kingsley Publishers Ltd.

Love L. & Stulberg J. (1996), Practice Guidelines for Co-Mediation, Making Certain That Two Heads Are Better Than One. *Mediation Quarterly,* 13, p179-189

Mayer B.S. (2004) *Beyond Neutrality, Confronting the Crisis in Conflict Resolution* San Francisco: Jossey-Bass

Menkel-Meadow C. (1993), Theories and Realities what we Learn from Mediation *The Modern Law Review,* 56(3), p361-379

Menkel-Meadow C. (1995) The Many Ways of Mediation: The Transformation of Traditions, Ideologies, Paradigms and Practices. *Negotiation Journal,* 11(3), p217-242

Merry S. (1993) Sorting out Popular Justice. In Merry S. & Milner N. (1993) *The Possibility of Popular Justice: A Case Study of Community Mediation in the United States* USA: The University of Michigan Press

Merry S. & Milner, N. (1993) *The Possibility of Popular Justice: A Case Study of Community Mediation in the United States,* USA: The University of Michigan Press

Meyer J.F. (2002) "It is a Gift from the Creator to Keep Us in Harmony:" Original (vs. Alternative) Dispute Resolution on the Navajo Nation. *International Journal of Public Administration,* 25(11), p1379-1401

Mischel W. (1993) *Introduction to Personality, 5th Edition* Orlando: Harcourt Brace Jovanovich College Publishers

Morrill C. & McKee C. (1993) Institutional Isomorphism and Informal Social Control: Evidence from a Community

Mediation Centre. *Social Problems,* 40(4), p445-463

Mulcahy L. & Summerfield L. (2001) *Keeping it in the Community: An Evaluation of the use of mediation in disputes between neighbours,* Norwich: Her Majesty's Stationery Office

Picard C. (2002) Common Language, Different Meaning: What Mediators Mean When They Talk About Their Work. *Negotiation Journal,* 18(3), p251-269

Pinzon L.A. (1996) The Production of Power and Knowledge in Mediation: *Mediation Quarterly,* 14(1), p3-20

Strasser F. & Randolph P. (2004) Mediation, *A Psychological Insight into Conflict Resolution,* London: Continuum Books

Susskind L.E. (2000) Confessions of a Public Dispute Mediator. *Negotiation Journal,* 16(2), p129-132

Yarn D.P. (2000) Conflict Management in Cross Cultural Perspective in Aureli F. & De Waal F.B.M. (2000). *Natural Conflict Resolution* California: University of California Press

Wehr, P. & Lederach, J.P. (1991), Mediating Conflict in Central America. *Journal of Peace Research,* 28(1), p85-98

Part 1: Philosophical background to co-mediation

3. Co-mediation: A very visible model of working with 'the other'

Monica Hanaway

Introduction

The mediator's neutrality and ability to form a respectful and trusting relationship with each party is one of the key factors in mediation. If the mediator uses a psychological approach with the parties, as explored in chapter 1 then this same awareness should also be present in the relationship between mediator and co-mediator. Conflict is part of all relationships. The fact that one person is the mediator and the other the co-mediator, could lead to hidden and unexpressed conflicts within the relationship.

Conflicts often ensue when we experience others as different to ourselves. The 'opponent' in a dispute takes on an alien aspect and we struggle to find connection. This sense of 'otherness,' is often experienced as scary and negative, reminiscent of Lacan's 'Other'[1] or Jung's 'Darkness'[2].

---

1 Lacan's use of 'other' follows Hegel; The little other is the other who is not really other, but a reflection and projection of the Ego. He [autre] is simultaneously the counterpart and the specular image. The little other is thus entirely inscribed in the imaginary order.

2. The big Other designates radical alterity, an other-ness which transcends the illusory otherness of the imaginary because it cannot be assimilated through identification. Lacan equates this radical alterity with language and the law, and hence the big Other is inscribed in the order of the symbolic. Indeed, the big Other *is* the symbolic insofar as it is particularized for each subject. The Other is thus both another subject, in his radical alterity and unassimilable uniqueness, and also the symbolic order which mediates the relationship with that other subject."

Jung's **'darkness'** speaks of the **shadow** or **"shadow aspect"**, a part of the unconscious mind consisting of instinctual and irrational projection – repressed weaknesses, shortcomings, and instincts. Jung believed that "Everyone carries a shadow and the less it is embodied in the individual's conscious life, the blacker and denser it is.' It may be linked to more primitive animal instincts which are superseded during early childhood by the conscious mind.

Co-mediators through their facilitation of a dispute show how two individuals with differing worldviews can come together, using different perspectives on the dispute to create movement and creative change. The co-mediators may well see things differently from each other, they may overtly disagree but their differences are used to add richness to the resolution.

The chapter will explore the concept of 'otherness' and the fear and anger this can produce. It starts with the assumption that the co-mediators will, just like the parties, have different reactions to aspects of the dispute and the personalities and behaviours of all of those involved. It will show the positive, creative side of *being* 'other' and of *encountering* and *engaging* with the other.

In engaging with otherness, commonalities are often discovered and it is this discovery which often unlocks the conflict and allows movement towards a resolution.

What do the co-mediators bring into mediation?

We have seen in the first chapter that each of the parties in the mediation bring with them aspects which are unique to themselves as individuals and which collectively we may term their 'worldview'. Just as each of the disputing parties brings their differences into the mediation room so too do co-mediators.

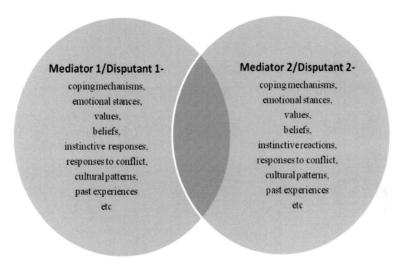

Fig 3.1 The worldviews of those participating in the mediation

We each bring to every experience coping strategies and behaviours which we consider have worked for us in the past. For example, one person may believe that taking a leadership role is a brave action which earns them respect, and that people are less likely to challenge a 'leader'. Others may equally strongly believe the opposite, seeing those who voluntarily take up a leadership role as pushy, possibly insecure individuals, who dare not offer their views to others in case they are challenged.

Whether mediator or disputant we will each arrive at the mediation with views as to what a just outcome may look like, we may find that we instinctively trust or like one of the individuals involved whilst disliking another. We will also have responses to being in a conflict. We have seen in the first chapter these can be very different ranging from a love of conflict and a desire for (or even addiction to) the adrenaline rush which it may bring. This may cause some individuals to seek it out and try to sustain it whilst others are so conflict averse that they will free or seek to run from it always seeking to acquiesce and to subordinate their needs to those of others

These thoughts and behaviours stem from our own values and beliefs and our unique life experiences.

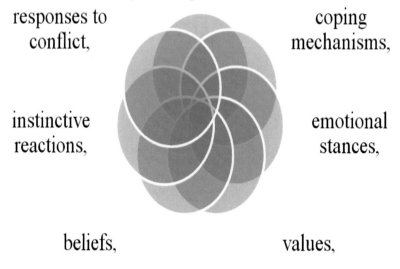

responses to
conflict,

coping
mechanisms,

instinctive
reactions,

emotional
stances,

beliefs,

values,

Fig 3.2 The complex interaction of worldviews at play in any mediation

If we stop to consider the complexity of the meetings of minds, each with their unique, multifaceted and intriguing worldviews, which exist in each mediation, we may be very put off from ever attempting to mediate. We may also ask, 'why add to the complications by have two mediators instead of one?'

The otherness of the co-mediator

Mediators who chose to work with another mediator generally do so for a number or reasons but mainly because they believe it to be a more positive experience for themselves as mediators and for the disputing parties in the mediation.

Co-mediators accept that they are different from one another and that those different experiences, styles and perspectives add to the richness of the mediating experience. One mediator may be more finely attuned to certain aspects of the dispute, one may have specialist knowledge and/or experience, the mediator's gender, race, sexual orientation or cultural belonging may also differ from that of their co-mediator and impact, for good or bad on the mediation experience.

In one mediation, where I was working with a male co-mediator we were faced with a party who seemed keen for us to see him as a successful, macho businessman who was not willing to give an inch to make the mediation work. Instead he saw the opportunity to show his greater financial power by forcing the other party through the court system, bankrupting him in the process and making a very unpleasant end to what had been a successful business partnership. I and my co-mediator were struggling to find any movement from this stance. After many hours my colleague excused himself to use the toilet and during that time the party visibly relaxed, sat lower in his chair, reached into his pocket and brought out a photograph of a small girl – his daughter, taken many years earlier. He then started to tell me how he was now divorced and not allowed contact with his daughter, who lived abroad with his ex-wife. He was clearly moved as he told me of the pain and hurt he had suffered. On hearing my co-mediator returning, he quickly put away the photograph, sat upright in his chair, once again, and was ready to do battle. My co-mediator and I were able to discuss what happened during a break and to use this new knowledge to understand that the party wanted us to be aware of his more emotional side but did not feel able to express it in the presence of another man. Here the fact that the co-mediators were a male and a female allowed something to be expressed which was very unlikely to have happened in the presence of one or two male mediators. It is my own view that it was also unlikely that he would have expressed this if working with two female mediators as the exposure may have felt too great.

In order to facilitate the mediation, any mediator has to be aware of the level of difference between participants, and the level of difference between herself and her co-mediator, with all the possibilities this may present for projection and projective identification; seeing one party as the bad, mad or dangerous element in the room, and thus holding the capacity for one person to become the 'scapegoat', carrying everyone's potential negativity.

An example of conflict

Working from the theoretical approach outlined above, I wish to examine one example of conflict and explore the ways in which individuals can become detached from the commonality of their shared human existence and focus instead on their difference from the other – their essential 'otherness.

As we have seen earlier in this chapter, in addition to the differences between the two people in dispute, the two co-mediators bring their own differences into the mediation

Together with another co-mediator I was asked to co-mediate between two people Jason (an Afro-Caribbean man) and Pat, (a Caucasian woman), who had to work with each other in a highly charged creative environment. Both were approximately the same age and held the same level of power within their organization. My co-mediator on this occasion was male and we both are white British. Our model of co-mediating was one were we both took equal responsibility; there was no 'lead' mediator.

The working relationship between the disputants had broken down following an allegation by another white female worker, Sue, (a close friend of the Pat's), of serious sexual harassment of her by Jason. Sue had refused to go ahead with the disciplinary hearing, claiming she was too afraid to do so. Both Jason and Pat were aware that they had to continue to work together or one of them would need to leave.

Vuchinich (1990) suggested that conflicts might be resolved by five different methods: compromise, third-party intervention, withdrawal, standoff, and submission. In this case, neither party was originally willing to compromise and instead had chosen to withdraw from each other, refusing to speak to one another thus creating a standoff and a desire to avoid submission. In this case, we were brought in to offer a third party intervention.

If we look to Jensen-Campbell, Graziano, & Hair's (1996) suggestion that in practice there are three outcomes: negotiated resolution (compromise and third-party resolution), disengagement (withdrawal and standoff), and coercion (submission), then we see that here disengagement could not be sustained and both parties were fighting against compromise or submission.

If we find a way to empathise with the other then fighting often ceases. However, in order to feel empathy we have first to 'meet' ourselves in the other. It is not easy to feel empathic towards someone or something we experience as alien. In this case, the 'otherness' of each party was very evident; gender, class, race, different cultural and moral codes. Sgubini (2006) states that,

> *'Mediation is a tool that helps to 'bridge the gap between differences and this requires knowing and respecting the culture of people that you meet... it is important for the mediator to understand how parties communicate. When carrying on an international mediation or even a domestic mediation with diverse parties. A mediator must take the cultural differences into consideration.'*

In order to facilitate the mediation, the mediators have to be aware of the level of difference between participants, with all the possibilities this may present for projection and projective identification, and the potential for identification of one party as bad, dark, unknown and therefore threatening.

In the opening statements, Jason's anger was very apparent. He stated he was so angry with Pat that he felt like attacking her. He shouted about how white people always thought of black men as 'sexual ogres, rapists, out of control'. He immediately touched on the sense of otherness he felt and which he believed others experienced in relation to him.

As I stated, I am a white woman and my co-mediator in this case a white man. Both Jason and Pat had known this when they agreed to the mediation. We also drew attention to these differences at the start of the mediation and checked that Jason felt OK about both mediators being white. He responded, rather angrily that that was what he was used to ... being the only black person in a meeting. We acknowledged that even if that was a common situation for him it was potentially difficult and asked that if at any time either party felt uncomfortable for any reason that they made this known to us.

In having male and female co-mediators we were hoping to equalize any sense of gender inequality that either party may have felt in being faced with a sole mediator of either gender or co-mediators of the same gender. In sexual harassment cases I believe that the opportunity presented by having male and female co-mediators is important.

In this case race was clearly an issue for Jason who believed that people, in particular women, chose to see him as an archetypal, stereotypical sexually aggressive black man. This has been explored by a number of writers both white and black. Fanon (1986), himself a black African, describes how white culture identifies the black man with the 'dark', 'animal' quality it fears in its own sexuality,

> *'European civilization is characterized by the presence, at the heart of what Jung calls the collective unconscious, of an archetype: an expression of the bad instincts, of the darkness inherent in every ego, of the uncivilized savage, the Negro that slumbers in every black man.'*

Kovel (1995), warns of the tendency for a psychic ghettoization into different kinds of being: sex roles, general roles, social roles in general, to take place and Altman (2003), describes how,

> *'black people represent the objectified human being...*
> *suitable containers for our sense of oppression'*

Zizek (1989), goes further, focusing on some of what may be feared in this objectification,

> *'We always impute to the 'other' an excessive*
> *enjoyment... what bothers us about the 'other' is the*
> *peculiar way he organizes his enjoyment'*

As co-mediators we believed that we needed to understand and take into account Jason's worldview and his emotional response to it, exploring the importance of how he saw himself and the contrast with how he experienced others seeing him. This was regardless of any personal reactions I or my co-mediator might have to the details of the allegation of sexual harassment. It was also a challenge as neither my co-mediator nor I had grown up as a member of a minority community. We knew that this meant we had to take great care to make no assumptions and to check that we were understanding as fully as possible how each individual had experienced the dispute, knowing that each would bring learning from their past experiences into what had happened.

In these emotive mediations, which we often find in workplace conflicts, I believe that it is important to understand the values, beliefs and behaviours of one's co-mediator. In this case we were reacting to the experiences of the disputants from within our own experiences as a white man and a white woman. These experiences inform our worldviews and therefore what we bring into the mediation. In this case we were also both bringing into the mediation the fact that we had lived life as members of the white majority. We could model cooperation across gender but not across race. We had discussed these elements of the dispute before meeting the parties. We were very aware of the danger that Jason may look to my co-mediator as an ally because of his gender and he may expect me to side with Pat, both being women. Throughout the mediation as co-mediators we were able to check in with one another and ensure no collusion or manipulation was taking place. This opportunity to act as informal supervisors and boundary holders for each other is an important quality which co-mediation brings.

Our task with Pat was to explore her emotional and ethical response to the situation. What was it that was important for her to come away from the mediation with? For the mediation to succeed we needed both parties to take the other's worldview into account. This was difficult, as it may have seemed that they had to give credence to the other's position when it fundamentally differed from their own. In Pat's case we were also asking that she see Jason as another person, with human vulnerabilities even though it was clear that she had dehumanized him and did not consider him to be worthy of respect or consideration.

There is not the space here to describe the mediation in full. However, it taught me an important lesson. After the first opening remarks, for which both were present and at which Jason made his outburst, we met separately with the parties. Pat told me that she was feeling much better! For her one of the things that she had found hardest to cope with was that the case had seemed to have no effect on Jason – 'he continued in his usual arrogant way, whilst Sue was distraught. ... I now see that he is really shaken by it and deeply upset ... that means a lot'.

I asked myself how easy would it have been just to hear Jason's outburst in the opening session, without being threatened, if I was mediating alone? Having another mediator in the room with me not only allowed me to sit with the discomfort I was feeling but also made me more confident.

Throughout the mediation my co-mediator and I attempted to model a cooperative working relationship. We did not agree on everything and were able to question one another in the mediation, in the presence of the disputants in ways which showed that difference can be allowed and indeed be viewed creatively e.g. 'Oh its interesting you see it that way, I was thinking...' being responded to with 'I hadn't thought of that, let me think about it and see whether that alters my view...' Each of us received the comments and interventions of the other mediator from a place of respect and interest in the difference their observation offered. We sought to do the same with both Pat and Jason, listening attentively and respectfully to both in equal measure.

Jason's growing feeling of trust in both mediators, believing that they were not going to side with either party against the other, allowed him to share some distressing past experiences with Pat. He told of how he often saw women cross the street if he were walking behind them (in his view this was because they feared his blackness and his maleness) and how he believed that what was considered harmless flirting from a white male was seen as sexual aggression from a black man. Pat conceded that she had never thought of this and could understand Jason's sensitivity on this point, however she was clear that she still believed that he had behaved inappropriately towards Sue and not expressed any contrition. Jason was able to express his sorrow over how what had happened had been interpreted and saw how his subsequent behaviour may have looked arrogant and as though he were untouched by what had happened.

At the end of the day, Jason and Pat left the mediation together and spent some time talking calmly in the car park. Although they will never be friends they are able to work together and behave professionally with one another.

Glasl's Conflict Model

Glasl (1999) offers a nine stage model to explore the development of conflict and we can see this in relation to Jason and Pat's experience.

Hardening

In the initial stages of this dispute both Pat and Jason felt they has tried to make their views known to the other but had failed to be listened to. As Glasl postulates, *'the standpoints attract adherents, and groups start to form around certain positions'*. In this case this was particularly disturbing as it split male/female, black/white. More effective interventions from management could have helped at this stage, but the manager was young and inexperienced and very worried about being seen as sexist or racist. Thus the *'habitual behaviour patterns'* of which Glasl writes began, firstly with verbal sparring then moved to a position where neither party believed in the humanity of the other or the possibility of resolution and so the conflict moved to stage two.

Debate and polemics

By now, both were *'locked into inflexible standpoints'*. The focus moved from the initial incident and began to focus on what each perceived to be the intrinsic personality of the other. Each chose to label the other with an 'ism'. For Pat, Jason was sexist, whilst, for Jason, Pat was racist and both were portrayed by the other's followers as absurd. At this stage, if they had not shared common goals within their work it would be difficult to see how this would resolve.

Actions not words

From here, Jason and Pat refused to speak to or acknowledge each other, fitting Glasl's (1999) description,

> *'The parties start to see themselves as being held captives by external circumstances they cannot control. They therefore deny responsibility for the course of events.*

An increasing part of their own actions are regarded as necessary responses to the behaviour of the other.'

Images and Coalitions

This was followed by an increased reduction of the other to fixed stereotypical archetypes, by now *'the negative images are screens that occupy the field of vision whenever the parties meet each other'* thus denying the potential for change. Jason and Pat both tried to involve supporters in seeing these stereotypes in the other.

Loss of face

This very quickly moved into stage 5 with Jason, in particular feeling he was being seen *'through the mask of the other'*... *'being regarded in terms of angels and devils... one side representative of the good forces in the world ... the other... the destructive, subhuman and bestial force'* thus mirroring Fanon's (1986)*'uncivilised savage'* motif.

Strategies of threats / Limited destructive blows / Fragmentation of the Enemy

One could say that it was the threat of damaging action (i.e. the grievance procedure), which moved it to the next stages, creating *'a pressure to act rapidly and radically'*, with the desire to *'eliminate/destroy'* the other, by having management discipline, or ultimately sack, the other. They rapidly moved to a position where their primary desire was survival, wanting their view to be validated by the mediator and the other's view denied.

The mediation process seemed to prevent them moving into Glasl's final stage; **'Together into the abyss'**.

In this case, Chris and Jane had to continue to work together whatever happened. Following the line of the mediation plan, we made this common tie explicit at the start of the mediation. They were both committed to the work they did with young people and both acknowledged that the current situation was damaging it. We found it important to feed this shared belief system back to them throughout the sessions, thus maintaining their commonality and thus their connectedness. If I had been mediating alone the repetition may have been annoying, coming from two mediators, expressing it in different ways and at different points in the mediation served to draw attention to its importance to both parties.

Some mediators believe that emotions can disrupt negotiation. In this case, emotions were very highly charged. Neither party started the sessions with respect for the other, feelings of hatred were overtly expressed. Pat spoke of her fear of Jason, painting a strong picture of his 'otherness' during a private caucus. Jason felt shame about the original allegation leading him to *'fly into a defensive rage'*. The client's emotions provide a valuable tool with which to work, although we were concerned in this case about the impact Jason's opening statement may have had on Pat. The very calm presence of my male co-mediator brought Pat a sense of safeness around the male presence but also allowed Jason the freedom to express his experience of being male.

Many psychological minded mediators see the expression of emotion as a gift they can work with. Strasser & Randolph (2004), stress their importance,

> *'Every emotion is connected with the givens, and each emotion is a manifestation is an aspect of people's worldview. Indeed, emotions are most useful tools for the mediator and for the parties to gain insight into aspects of their own worldview...they can highlight some of the ambivalences each party holds...'*

Thomas Scheff (1991), draws our attention particularly to the emotion 'shame', with his 'core sequence' in 'emotional conciliation' requiring that one party expresses shame or remorse and that the other 'takes the first step towards forgiving the offender'. Although not disagreeing with this I believe it is important to consider what shame means within the culture of the individual. My belief is that for some cultures it is easier to express shame than in others. If we look to shame one party and elicit forgiveness form the other party, then we create an additional 'otherness'. In my view, it is more important to create a sense of commonality between the conflicting parties that opposes and, eventually, nullifies the alienation, or tendency to see the other disputant as 'THE OTHER'. In this case both Jason and Pat felt aggrieved, both were worried about losing their job if they could not find a way of working together and both had become frightened of the other.

Jason had very clearly become 'the other', He felt he was not seen by Pat as fully human, merely a stereotype and so not to be trusted, or deserving of equal treatment. He was a black belt at judo and believed that you defended yourself through attack and his racial, cultural and class background meant that he saw an admission to vulnerability as a failing in his masculinity. This meant that we had to explicitly demonstrate impartiality and fairness throughout the process, ensuring that both parties had equal opportunities to express their views and these were held to be equally important. It was also important that as a male and female co-mediator we were equally active and neither taking a more prominent role than the other. Jason clearly did not feel safe when he agreed to the mediation and we were careful to choose a neutral venue to which both parties agreed and to make the non-judgemental aspect of our role clear. It was also essential that we maintained Jason's self-esteem even when we challenged him as to possible outcomes if he stuck rigidly to his current stance. At the same time Pat needed to experience both of us taking her seriously and believing in the level of anger and fear she expressed.

What Jane required for a successful resolution was very different from what I or my co-mediator had anticipated. For her it was good enough that she had seen that Jason had been affected by the allegation. This emphasized for me the importance of the mediators being truly open and bracketing their own assumptions.

On the surface, both parties had equal power. They were at the same level within their organization. However, both felt power imbalances in relation to their gender and race and these played an important part in the dispute and needed to be gently explored in order to resolve the conflict. In the one to one sessions it was apparent that both considered that despite doing work they liked, others might consider them to have failed because they had not 'progressed' into management. Both held a need to be superior to the other, and in the eyes of the mediators.

The mediation allowed both Pat and Jason to truly express their concerns including some difficult feelings and perceptions which each held towards the other and to identify points of commonality. Breaking through this deception and secrecy allowed the real issues to be discussed. Pat's fear of Jason subsided once she had seen his vulnerability. She was then able to treat him as a fellow human being, thus removing one of his major grievances. I believe having male and female co-mediators helped this to happen.

Both parties had clearly hoarded up negative perceptions about each other. These feelings were safely yet fully explored and thus changed to a degree thus making it possible for them to work together in the future.

My own belief is that the majority of conflicts, although perhaps starting with an objective disagreement, become enmeshed by virtue of identity issues and individual value sets, which need to be respectfully explored. This is true of both individual and small and large group conflicts. The presence of two mediators with different backgrounds, sets of values and beliefs, coping strategies and behavior patterns yet working together for a shared outcome demonstrates that 'otherness' can be creative as well as collaborative. A sole mediator, may help the parties to address the conflict creatively and work collaboratively towards a solution, but is not in a position to show this happening in a concrete way.

References

Altman N., (2003), How white people suffer from white racism. In *Psychotherapy & Politics International,* 1(2)

Fanon F., (1986), *'Black Skin, White Masks'* London: Pluto Press

Freud S., (1930) *'Civilisation and Its Discontents',* Penguin Freud Library, London: Penguin 1985

Glasl F., (1999), *'Confronting Conflict',* Bristol: Hawthorn Press

Grimshaw (Ed.), *'Conflict talk: Sociolinguistic investigations of arguments in conversations'* (pp. 118–138). New York: Cambridge Univ. Press.

Hicks. T., (1996-2000), Seven steps for effective problem-solving in the workplacehttp//www.conflict-resolution.net/articles/index.cfm edn.

Jensen-Campbell, L. A., Graziano, W. G., & Hair, E. C. (1996), *'Personality and relationships as moderators of interpersonal conflict in adolescence'.* Merrill-Palmer Quarterly, 42, 148–164.

Kovel J., (1995). On Racism and Psychoanalysis, in Elliot A. & Frosch S. (eds), *'Psychoanalysis in Contexts'* London: Routledge

Liebmann M (ed.)., (2000), *'Mediation in Context',* London: Jessica Kingsley Publishers

Reich W., (1967), *'Reich speaks of Freud',* London: Condor

Sacks, J., (2002), *'The Dignity of Difference'*, London: Continuum

Samuels A.., (1993), *'The Political Psyche'*, London: Routledge

Scheff T, Retzinger S. *'Emotions* and *Violence'*. Lexington, MA: Lexington Books; 1991.

Sgubini A., (2006), ' *Mediation and Culture: How different cultural backgrounds can affect the way people negotiate and resolve disputes'*, – http://www.mediate.com/articles/sugbini

Strasser F. & Randolph P., (2004*), 'Mediation – A Psychological Insight into Conflict Resolution'*, London: Continuum.

Suttie I., (1936), *'The Origins of Love and Hate,'* Harmondsworth: Penguin

Totton N., (2006), *'The Politics of Psychotherapy"*, Maidenhead: Open University Press

Vuchinich, S. (1990). 'The sequential organization of closing in verbal family conflict'. In A. D. Grimshaw (Ed.), *'Conflict talk: Sociolinguistic investigations of arguments in conversations'* (pp. 118–138). New York: Cambridge Univ. Press.

Zizek S., (1989), *'The Sublime Object of Ideology'*, London: Verso

4. Is Co-Mediation Better for Parties and Mediators?

Diana Mitchell

Introduction

When I first qualified as a mediator I assumed that the majority of mediators worked alone and not with another mediator. I also found it difficult to imagine how two mediators would work together and I worried that the parties might find it confusing to talk to two mediators at the same time. I have worked with couples as a psychotherapist and I naively assumed that mediation would be very similar; two people who want to find a way to resolve their conflict. I had not taken into account that in couple therapy I meet once a week with the couple, either together or in separate sessions and that our contract is open-ended or for an agreed time in the near future, whereas in mediation I would only have one day. In couple therapy the couple and the therapist have a week between sessions – in mediation everything seems to happen in that one day.[3] The parties will each have time alone while the mediator is with the other party to think their situation through, but it often happens that the mediator gives him or herself very little time alone during the mediation to take stock and digest what is happening.

I mediated on my own when I first started mediating, but it was only when I started working as a co-mediator that I discovered first-hand how important it was for mediators to be able to support each other during a mediation. When mediating alone I realized that my greatest enemy was fatigue.

---

3   Some community and family mediation models differ in that meetings are spread over a period of days or weeks

Obviously fatigue affects how we think and thinking clearly and calmly is crucial for mediators. The mediators' function is to try to find a way to facilitate a shift in the parties' attitude towards each other and their dispute while being mindful not to push their own solutions at the parties. The mediator I co-mediate with acts as lead mediator in that she organizes the mediation, books the rooms and deals with all the pre-mediation issues.

However once we start mediating we work as 'equals' with the parties. We have a very good working relationship, which is built on trust and an appreciation of each other's different qualities. And more importantly, neither of us is at our best when we get over tired! All the mediations I have done are time-limited workplace mediations.

Time-limited mediation in a workplace situation presents an interesting dilemma for mediators and parties alike. The parties and their mediator(s) have one day to find a 'good enough' way to resolve their dispute. I believe that the deadline acts as a motivator for the parties to resolve or possibly not resolve their conflict on the day. However, this deadline, particularly towards the end of the mediation can cause the mediator to be 'hijacked by time' and to become a directive leader rather than facilitative follower. Mediators need to continue to have what I call 'blind faith in the process' right up to the end of the day and let the parties have the last word and take responsibility for the outcome, while also doing everything possible to facilitate a shift in the parties attitude towards each other and their conflict.

Other characteristics of many work place mediations are that there tend to be power issues between the two parties and that one of the parties has often been 'forced' to attend and is therefore very reluctant to get involved in the process.

Mediations are emotional for parties and mediators

It is not possible to be in conflict or have an argument with someone and remain indifferent and unemotional and it is very difficult to be involved with two people who are distressed and emotional while remaining detached yourself. The mediator and co-mediator will be thrown into the parties' conflict; they will be affected by the parties' anger, distress, frustration and fear – some of the many emotions that come into play during mediations.

The mediator's main task is to listen and to clearly demonstrate a good understanding of the parties' predicament, how it has affected them emotionally and what they feel they need in order to move forward.

Being non-judgmental, empathizing and demonstrating understanding to and with each party all play their part in facilitating open and honest self-expression by the parties.

The mediator's ability to facilitate and follow the parties throughout the mediation process plays an important part in helping each party to see that they will have to work something out together that will be acceptable to them both. It is not the mediator's task to come up with solutions or to assume to know what the outcome 'should' be.

This would sound straightforward enough if it were not for the fact that it is impossible to be neutral or non-judgmental. Our judgments, points of view and values make us who we are, so we cannot ignore them, but we must be aware of at least some of them. We will respond to the parties differently and possibly warm to one party more than the other.

The mediator will then need to find a way to 'bracket' (Spinelli, E. 1989:17) or put aside his or her feelings and personal beliefs if they seem to be competing with the parties' 'lived experience'. By temporarily setting our views to one side we will hopefully be more able to truly listen to and focus on the parties and their views, feelings and aspirations rather than on our own.

No matter how hard we try, our views will slip out from time to time; we will catch ourselves leading rather than following (albeit in a very subtle way) and our bodies will possibly express our feelings. This often happens in time-limited mediation when we start watching the clock and/or when the parties and we are becoming frustrated and tired. Having a co-mediator helps us to spot when this happens.

Our natural way of listening to someone is to get caught up in our own assumptions and views and to want to impose these on the person we are listening to. In fact, what we are doing is going through the motions of listening on the surface: *'There's a big difference in showing interest and really taking interest'* (Nichols, M.P. 1995: 74-81) expresses this beautifully.

As human beings we do not get to know and understand each other through dialogue alone; we watch and pick up clues visually, we also get a 'felt sense', a term used by Eugene Gendlin (Preston, L. 2008) to describe vague bodily feelings that can be hard to articulate and yet these feelings also inform our overall impression and understanding.

Mediation and supervision

I hope that I have over the years cultivated a 'good enough' internal supervisor. By that I mean my ability to have a self-reflective dialogue with myself. But this does not mean that I don't at times need another person to talk to about my various mediation relationships. There can be a big difference between thinking I am being silently self- aware and the kind of awareness that comes from talking to and with another person.

After I have mediated on my own I am left with a burning need to take stock and talk through my experience of the day with another mediator. Mediators are at present not required to have supervision, which I find puzzling given that mediators are caught up in relationships with their parties and have a need to talk through any concerns they may have about how they managed the mediation.

I recognize that I have not always found the time or energy for self-reflective dialogue during my lone mediations, particularly towards the end of the mediation where energy levels are low, emotions have flared up and time seems to be running out.

The unexpected will always happen which means that the mediator needs to be flexible and be able to make judgment calls. But when working with another mediator both mediators can use each other as sounding boards for their impressions, feelings, and concerns, and to consider the bigger picture. Each mediator witnesses the other mediator in relation to the parties and might see something that only an outsider can notice. Each mediator acts as a witness to the other. I see this partnership as a 'multi-dimensional' relationship where each mediator can become more self-aware 'through the eyes of the other'. We each continue to have our internal supervisors, but added to that is an external supervisor who can help us to watch and judge ourselves in a more disciplined way.

Time-limited mediation surrounded by uncertainty

The mediations that I have been involved in take place within an agreed time, usually one day. The mediation starts with a clear deadline. What happens within that time frame is cloaked in uncertainty for the mediator; the mediator has no idea how or if the parties will resolve their dispute. The parties will also feel the uncertainty factor and possibly start to lose confidence in their mediators. Uncertainty at the beginning of mediation can imply 'hope', but towards the end of mediation this hope can be replaced by despair. The process is not linear or logical; the parties can suddenly swing from coming close to an agreement to being as far apart as they were at the beginning of the mediation.

The mediator will possibly have to remind the parties throughout that they are ultimately responsible for the outcome. I am not convinced that the parties really want to believe that they have to find their own solution. I believe that they will continue to see the mediator(s) as 'the experts', the professionals who will give them sound advice and point them in the right direction. Added to this, it is almost humanly impossible for mediators not to in some way 'feel' responsible for the outcome, particularly when the parties put pressure on the mediators to find a solution. No mediator wants to have too many unresolved mediations under his or her belt.

A mediator working alone will not only have a dialogue with the parties but a vitally important, on-going dialogue with him or herself; making time to take mini breaks between the private sessions to think through what is happening and how best to proceed.

A lone mediator will also have to be aware of time and yet try not to rush the parties; 'rushing the parties' is often an indication that the mediator is starting to take responsibility for the outcome, particularly towards the end of the day. Solution focused questions from the mediator can start to slip in (Strasser & Randolph, 2004:138) if the going starts to get tough near the end.

The above will also happen to two mediators working together, but the experience is obviously different when it is shared.

I believe that two mediators working together are more likely to monitor and deal with their own and each other's and the parties' 'wellbeing' during the mediation and they will be able to share and compare how they understand and 'see' the parties and their conflict. While one mediator is talking to a party the other mediator will have time to silently reflect while listening to the dialogue between the party and the other mediator.

They will be able to consult each other, witness each other in action and most importantly feel satisfied that together they have given their all and that the parties have been given a worthwhile experience, no matter what the outcome might be.

As mediators we will do our utmost to ensure the comfort and trust of the parties by showing consideration, respect and acceptance of each party's particular needs throughout. The parties will feel 'unsafe' if they don't trust or have confidence in their mediator, or if they feel in any way that the mediator is trying to manipulate them. This all-important trust can be lost at any time throughout the mediation and when that happens the mediator needs to explore what has happened for the party and find a way to regain their trust. A mediator and co-mediator can work out how to regain the parties' trust together, each using their different sensitivities.

Mediators should also not forget their own comfort and well-being, which could affect the parties, the outcome and their mediation experience as a whole. It seems to me that co-mediation can be better for both parties and mediators.

References:

Nicols M.P. (1995) *The Lost Art of Listening* The Guildford Press: New York

Preston L. (2008) *The Edge of Awareness, Gendlin's Contribution to Explorations of the Implicit* http://www.focusing.or/fot/The%20Edge%20fo20awareness.pdf

Spinelli E. (1998) *The Interpreted World – An Introduction to Phenomenological Psychology* Sage Publications Ltd

5. Unlearning in Co-Mediation Training, Practice and Participation -What makes the Possible a Possibility

Jamie Reed

Introduction

As co-mediators in training and practice, as well as for disputant parties in a co-mediation, there is an essential process that must take place. This is the process of unlearning. Unlearning is the process by which we can challenge our assumptions, can come to consider exceptions and explore new possibilities. New possibilities about how we see ourselves, others and the world.

For training co-mediators the unlearning is around developing new skills and an understanding of how co-mediation works for them. For disputants in a co-mediation it is about unlearning assumptions and behaviours so the meaning they attribute to their values can be re-considered. While for qualified co-mediators this is about the on-going unlearning needed to develop their capacity to practice as a co-mediator.

What is interesting about co-mediation is the extra dimension to the unlearning due to the presence of an additional mediator. Essentially there is another set of assumptions and values in the room. This extra dimension presents both potential challenges and opportunities to all involved in co-mediation. While it is the unlearning process that allows all concerned to take advantage of this extra dimension. Unlearning creates the space for new understanding of what is possible for us, for the world we experience and the conflicts we encounter.

So as the title suggests unlearning makes the possible a possibility for all involved in co-mediation. How unlearning works in these three contexts of co-mediation is the focus of this chapter.

Values and Assumptions

> '*To err is human. Yet most of us go through life assuming (and sometimes insisting) that we are right about nearly everything, from the origins of the universe to how to load the dishwasher. If being wrong is so natural, why are we all so bad at imagining that our beliefs could be mistaken, and why do we react to our errors with surprise, denial, defensiveness, and shame?*' (Schulz K. 2010 p 405)

Most of the time the assumptions we make about the world and the people we encounter serve to help us make sense of the world, to make choices in our lives and ultimately not live in a constant state somewhere between bewilderment and crippling anxiety.

At times, probably far more often than we like or could bear to acknowledge, the world and its populous don't play along. It suddenly becomes very difficult to interpret our experience as being congruent with our assumptions and beliefs. We are in conflict, in conflict with our beliefs about ourselves and the world as we see it. How this phenomenon is revealed, and the extent to which it is acknowledged, is different for all of us. What is universally true is that life is suddenly not so straight forward. Our assumptions don't fit.

Learning

The process of learning and indeed *unlearning* differs according to which religion, philosophical tradition or psychological writer you encounter. For the purpose of this chapter I shall be referring to the NLP Learning Levels as a framework for understanding learning. While for unlearning I will take what I see as a largely existential interpretation for the meaning of unlearning.

From an NLP perspective the learning process can be divided into four levels:

> 1) **Unconscious Incompetence:** You don't know and you don't know you don't know. Think of some activity you do well, such as reading, playing a sport or driving a car. Once upon a time you didn't know anything about it. You were not even aware of it.

> 2) **Conscious Incompetence:** Now you practice the skill, but you aren't very good. You learn fast at this stage though because the less you know the greater the room for improvement.

> 3) **Conscious Competence:** Here you have skill, but it is not yet consistent or habitual. You need to concentrate. This is a satisfying part of the learning process, but improvement is more difficult. The better you are the more effort is required to make a noticeable gain.

> 4) **Unconscious Competence:** Now your skill is habitual and automatic. You don't have to think about it. This is the goal of learning, to put as much of that skill as possible into the realms of unconscious competence, so your conscious mind is free to do something else, for example, talk to the passengers and listen to music while driving a car. (O'Conner, 2001. p.24)

What is interesting about these levels is that they focus on the learning of a new skill without considering the relationship, tension and conflict between our existing beliefs and assumptions and the new or different knowledge we are trying to acquire. What this chapter will be focusing on in particular is stage 2 of the Learning Levels to explore and unpack what takes place from an existential perspective. In particular I will be focusing on the notion of 'room for improvement' as described above that can be created with *unlearning*. I will be positing that this room or space is existential uncertainty that pervades all our lives. It is through the process of unlearning that uncertainty is revealed and space created for new possibility, new knowledge and new skills. Conversely therefore without unlearning, no new possibility is possible. Without possibility there is no change, no development of understanding, no capacity to reach resolution to disputes or to work successfully as a co-mediator.

Unlearning

In the first instance it is probably easier to say what unlearning isn't. It is not about negation, what Freud called *die verneinung* of what you know, or indeed facing that what you believe is 'wrong.' It is more that there are other interpretations of a situation that are equally 'true'. This position is mirrored by one of the guiding principles of mediation that we do not ask disputants to give up their values just to consider them in a new way, to include exceptions and/or other possibilities. Siff J. (2010) makes a similar point in reference to learning meditation,

> *'What you renounce while unlearning meditation is not any previously learned meditation technique but, rather, any strong intentions that may have been attached to the technique. It becomes possible to do the meditation practices with gentle intentions. If you've learned, for example, to follow the breath as a meditation practice, this approach isn't about abandoning that practice; rather, it's about doing it without a strong intention'.* (p.12)

What unlearning refers to is a process of accepting and embracing the consequences of the given that our lives are uncertain. What will happen in the future and our beliefs are not as concrete as we might think. Spinelli (2007) explains:

> '...existential uncertainty remains a constant given of human experience rather than revealing itself to be just an occasional and temporary consequence of unusual circumstances. It suggests that the structural point of view we make of self, others and the world in general is always incomplete, unfixed in any final shape or form- and, hence, uncertain. (p.25)

Within existential thought it is understood that at some level we are always aware of this underlying uncertainty but what differs is the strength of the intentionality which these assumptions held. Fundamentally our assumptions serve as a strategy for coping with this uncertainty. The difficulty being that what we gain in terms of a sense of psychological 'safety' we lose in our capacity to embrace the possibility for new learning, new experience, new understanding and to resolve conflicts.

Unlearning in Co-Mediation Training: Creating the 'space' of Uncertainty

The more I learn, the more I learn how little I know. –
Socrates

As a student training to be a co-mediator being asked to take on new knowledge and acquire new skills is inevitable. This presents a potential challenge and conflict for the student between the knowledge they bring to the class and the new knowledge and skills that must be acquired to be a co-mediator. From an existential perspective what will determine the extent of the challenge for the student is the level of intention with which they hold their existing knowledge and so resist the space for the unlearning process and the uncertainty that is revealed.

As outlined, strong beliefs can have a profound impact on our ability to develop new understanding and skills. The more rigorously the beliefs are held, the more difficult it can be to receive challenge, to consider new possibilities and so develop a broader understanding. If students are to learn something new it is essential to make space for the possibility that we have more or different things to learn. This requires an acceptance that what we know may not always be true. Without this transition it is likely that the student will find it difficult to engage with the training. Gestalt psychotherapy describes such knowledge as a *negative introject*:

> ...'a belief, idea or feeling in relation to the self (or the self in relationship to others) which interferes with the individual's ability to positively and freely contact the environment (Nevis E. p.99)

It is this ability/willingness to allow contact with our uncertain space that allows us to question our existing knowledge that is the essence of unlearning process.

It is perfectly possible that the new student might arrive having already started this process of unlearning by being open to uncertainty and challenge. This is not to say that they still not might find they are conflicted or challenged at times during the unlearning. The underlying principle is that the greater the acceptance and willingness to embrace uncertainty the greater the potential they have for unlearning and to develop co-mediation skills.

The nature of the knowledge and experience the student brings as well as how profoundly it is held can also impinge on the student's ability to unlearn and develop co-mediation skills. Specifically the student's current or previous career and the values they carry can be very influential. The obvious example being students from careers that allow very little space for uncertainty that rely heavily on facts; evidence based thinking and/or diagnostic frameworks. The notion of considering or working with uncertainty may well be deemed unprofessional, unethical or even dangerous. In this context unlearning or reframing what the student understands by professionalism, ethics and danger may be of value.

Working with the Assumptions

'Begin challenging your own assumptions. Your assumptions are your windows on the world. Scrub them off every once in a while, or the light won't come in'. – Alan Alda

It is part of the existential human condition to attempt to make definite the uncertainties of our experience. Paradoxically the more uncertain the circumstances are the more vehemently we can endeavor to consider our beliefs absolute. This paradox places us in intra-psychic conflict. This is an experience that can be potentially very uncomfortable to sit with but also has the potential to shine a light on something that is worthy of our attention. Acknowledging this uncomfortable feeling is the first part of the process of unlearning; by giving the feeling attention. The significance of this discomfort and the internal conflict it reveals is the 'tipping point' both of unlearning and conflict resolution.

Our response to this feeling of discomfort brought about by the conflict results in one of two responses *fight* or *fight*. These two modes of response where first coined by Bradford Cannon (1915). They describe the two survival methods we employ to defend our sense of self – our beliefs. This is survival of self from an existential perspective; as it is our beliefs that give us our sense of who we are.

What is essential again is the willingness and capacity of the student to question a) their emotional response- the uncomfortable feeling and b) the behaviour that goes hand in hand- fight or flight. The capacity to question with openness is key, what Bateson (1972) refers to as 'learning to learn' by questioning our assumptions.

Developing Unlearning in Co-Mediation Students

People are disturbed not by things, but by the view they take of them. – Epictetus

Within an existentially based approach to mediation training the majority of the course is experiential. Students are asked to both practice mediation skills but also play the parts of the disputants in accordance to confidential briefs. Following each of these sessions there is a facilitated plenary in which all participants are encouraged to reflect on their perspective and question their assumptions of the practice session. What is interesting about the practice and plenary sessions is that students are given a considerable amount of 'space' by the tutor to play the roles as the student interprets them according to their own assumptions. This is true whether they are the disputant parties or mediators in practice. It is by providing and maintaining this space that the tutor holds the uncertain space that purveys all existence. A space for uncertainty that means there is no definitive 'right or wrong' way to play the parts or indeed to mediate. This encounter with the space for uncertainty presents the student with an opportunity for unlearning.

Unlearning can be initiated through this experience of an uncertain space alone. To expand this potential opportunity it is part of the plenary process for tutors to facilitate the development of student's awareness of their unique process. Fundamentally this is done by encouraging students to reflect on how they went about the exercise, what assumptions they were making and what different possibilities might exist as alternative or additional ways to approach the exercise.

The process of having to play the roles of numerous different disputants is also important to the unlearning in mediation training. It encourages students to step into the shoes of the disputant and see the world from their perspective rather than their own. As a consequence the capacity of the student to immerse themselves into the character can give a good indication of their capacity for unlearning as this requires the same gentle intention towards values that is necessary for unlearning.

Developing Disputants Unlearning in Co-Mediation

'Everything that irritates us about others can lead us to an understanding of ourselves'. – Carl Jung

For people in dispute there exists a very similar intra-psychic conflict as described above. However it is often the parties' external conflict, the context, which is the focus for the parties rather than the intra-psychic conflict. What an existential co-mediation approach offers is an opportunity for parties to look beyond the circumstances and context of the conflict and explore their respective values that the conflict reveals. This exploration precedes the process of unlearning as it is first essential for co-mediators to develop a good deal of trust with the party. If a disputant is going to even consider new possibilities they must first trust that the co-mediators don't represent a threat to their values and sense of self. It is essential that their values will be respected and that they feel emotionally safe enough before unlearning is possible. At this level what co-mediation offers is an additional person willing to listen to them, keen to understand and work with them to resolution.

Although co-mediation is by no means a stage by stage process that could be seen as formulaic. There are definite phases to the unlearning process within co-mediation. These phases represent the realms of experience to be explored by the co-mediators. These realms are comprised of the values and meaning that the person attributes to the different areas of their experience of the conflict. Places for the co-mediators to explore and develop the parties understanding and learn more about the significance of their values in relation to the conflict. So that once the values pertinent to that realm have been clarified a starting point for possible unlearning can be established.

These realms are:

- The Self

- The Other (Other Disputants)

- The Conflict (The Relationship)

- The Future (The Resolution)

This notion of phases or realms should definitely have the caveat that if a party in mediation is particularly open from the start realms two, three and four are very much interchangeable. Indeed all the phases, after phase one, can be explored non-sequentially. What the phases do is serve as a guide rather than a systemic process. What is key is the importance of starting with the person and developing understanding of their personal values first. As mentioned this builds trust, preserves the ego and provides excellent bedrock for going on to exploring the other potentially more challenging realms.

From Learning to Unlearning

Part of what can hold a person in conflict can be their perception of being in the right in a unilateral sense. In addition it is not uncommon for parties to attempt try to convince a mediator they are in the right, get them to take their side or assume that the co-mediator agrees. There is of course a big gap between understanding the person position and agreeing with them.

Nonetheless these can be very important strategies for a disputant to help reinforce their misperception that their values are unilaterally held by all and as a way of coping with the underlying uncertainty. These strategies can also be significant barriers to unlearning. One of the potential benefits of the presence of two mediators can be that is can make employing these strategies harder. While co-mediators are clearly working together in a congruous and collaborative way they retain different perspectives and interpretations. This alone can make finding an ally in a mediator more difficult.

A co-mediator's initial focus is on helping the parties learn more about their individual values as the essential starting point to move into unlearning. The key skill employed in co-mediation to help parties learn more about their own values is called *tuning in*. Strasser & Randolph (2004) describe this process as:

> '...a form of 'associative involvement' with the other person, allowing himself put himself or herself into the other persons shoes- an empathic relationship involving the validation of the party by understanding his or her point of viewpoint [worldview].' (p.48)

Tuning in is intrinsic in helping disputants learning and subsequent unlearning. In order for co-mediators to put themselves in the shoes of the disputant they must endeavor to suspend their own values. By not imposing their values there is space for the party to explore and learn about their values without challenge. The co-mediator's perspective must be one of naivety and reassurance without initial reference to their perspective or assumptions. The hope being that by providing a safe space for this learning the party will in time will be open to unlearning, start to question their perspective and become open to other possible interpretations. It is this opening up that is the tipping point between learning and unlearning.

The Unlearning Process in Co-Mediation

"The most useful piece of learning for the uses of life is to unlearn what is untrue." – Antisthenes

The process of unlearning in co-mediation doesn't look to change the values of the parties merely to develop their capacity to:

• Develop awareness of their values

• Make safe the space to question these values

• Consider and accept possible exceptions that resolves the conflict

The process of co-mediation is facilitated by unlearning in a couple of ways. The first, as discussed, is by maintaining a space for values to be explored and challenged. What co-mediation adds is additional potential ways to explore these values and their exceptions. Not to say that one mediator is not sufficient to facilitate the unlearning process. More that by virtue of the mediators having similar but different interpretations means that they will each pick up on different strands of the conversation, potentially exploring unconsidered points. Different mediators are also likely to phrase their questions and interpretations differently. This gives the parties more than one perspective to work with. It is down to the co-mediators to ensure these differences and alternatives aren't just making the situation more confusing. It is essential for the co-mediator be tuned in to both the party and the co-mediator so as not to be coming in from left field. The process of mediation and unlearning can be very challenging and draining for disputants it is essential that co-mediators ensure they are not adding to this pressure.

Once a degree of trust has been established and learning has been initiated it is then possible to consider unlearning. To explore the exceptions and to challenge values. This element of the unlearning process is defined by considering and accepting other possibilities. Firstly, that there might be other possible ways to understand their situation. That it is possible that their original interpretation of the other person's behaviour might not have been completely accurate. That it is possible that the situation has had an emotional impact on all concerned. That it is possible that their own behaviour might have contributed to conflict and that it wasn't just about the other person being in the wrong.

The position taken by the co-mediators when attempting to develop unlearning more actively and creatively by being more challenging is called *tuning* out. Again referencing Strasser and Randolph (2004: 45) this skill is described as:

> '...when the mediator 'tunes out' from this associative mode [being tuned in], he or she enters into a more dynamic or active mode of intervention...'

This is not to suggest that unlearning cannot be facilitated when tuned in. Parties that are questioning the implications of their values can facilitate their own unlearning with very little challenge or need for dynamic or active intervention. In these circumstances just the maintenance of the space for exploration by the mediators is often sufficient.

Unlearning doesn't just constitute a process of broadening the meaning of the disputant's values. There are potential implications to behaviour resulting from these changes in meaning. By changing the way a situation is perceived it becomes possible to change the way we respond to it. If you stop seeing all spiders as something to be scared of, you can calmly remove the Money spider from you bath but still know a highly poisonous Red Back spider should be left alone. The same is true in mediation if you come to understand that everything the person you are in dispute isn't an attack you won't need to defend yourself. More than this though a space has been created to find out what it is the other person *is* actually trying to communicate. This is when unlearning is becoming a lived position.

If a party is able to adopt this position they can begin to tune in to the other party, to put themselves in their shoes and leave their own values alone for a few minutes. By taking such a position they can continue to develop the unlearning process beyond the mediation by being able to look upon themselves from the position of the other person. Here it becomes possible for them to see how hard it may have been for the other party and even how their behaviour contributed to maintaining the conflict.

Resolution: The Outcome of Unlearning in Co-Mediation

'In a time of drastic change, it is the unlearners who inherit the future. The learned find themselves equipped to live in a world that no longer exists'. – Eric Hoffer

The outcome of these adaptations of meaning and behaviour discussed above can alleviate the tension of the conflict. Instead the same space that was co-created by the mediators at an intra-psychic level within the parties can now exist in the relationship between the parties. This is a space that is open, collaborative and non-judgemental.

During the mediation process this space is often incredibly fragile but is required to 'go to work' very quickly in drawing up the Heads of Agreement (HOA). Parties at this point have a very tentative experience of this space and can easily fall back into their old assumptions. It is imperative for the co-mediators to hold the space that has been co-created during this stage. Staying with the unlearning process, re-affirming the value of what has been learnt as well as considering the consequences of regressing. The HOA despite constituting some potentially very practical, financial and/or legal elements represent the assumptions that the parties will share going forward. This is an essential frame of reference for the parties to maintain their unlearning process and build trust in their new view of the relationship.

Unlearning Co-Mediators in Practice

Unlearning between Co-Mediators

> *'Complacency provides a useful warning to those who think they have reached the limit of mastery. It can also encourage people to search for continuous improvement.'* John Addy

In order for co-mediators to work together successfully it is important that they too embrace the spirit and practice of unlearning at all times. It is the mediator's ability to be mindful of their own values and to embrace the space and possibility for both misinterpretation and reinterpretation of what is going on that allow unlearning to take place. The same is true for mediators practicing on their own. However in co-mediation there is an extra dimension to be considered, namely the assumptions in relationship between the co-mediators.

In response to this you might consider co-mediating with someone that you don't know might be easier as you have no historical relationship on which to base your assumptions. Unfortunately our assumptions about people are so far reaching that they encompass those we haven't even met. So our expectations and hopes of those we are yet to meet are subject to the same assumptions and require the same openness to unlearning.

On the flip side to this by working with someone that you have come to know trust in the uncertainty is essential between co-mediators. This is true in the same way as it is crucial between mediators and disputant parties. Ultimately if co-mediators are not willing to trust what each other does, even if they might not follow or understand it in the moment, they are not really embracing the space for uncertainty that unlearning requires. That is not to say that you cannot clarify, question or challenge a course of action between caucus sessions. Trust between co-mediators is not the same as blind faith.

Adopting a position of unlearning is an active process, a discipline for the co-mediator. It is not sufficient just to say that you are open. It is indicative of the co-mediators commitment to unlearning that they seek to explore and challenge assumptions at all stages in the mediation process. This can include in between the caucus sessions and following the mediation in the plenary.

There also exists space for unlearning at a theoretical and skill level for mediators too. A commitment to CPD (continuing professional development) is demonstrative not in its attendance as a box to tick for accreditation purposes or pier approval but in acknowledgement of the practice of unlearning. One has never arrived as a co-mediator. A successful co-mediator is in a perpetual state of moving towards, a movement towards mastery of unlearning.

References

Barford D. ed. (1997) *Lifelong Unlearning: The Ship of Thought. Essays on Psychoanalysis and Learning'*, (London: Karnac Books)

Bradford-Cannon W. (1915) Bodily Changes in Pain, Hunger, Fear and Rage: An Account of Recent Researches into the Function of Emotional Excitement: *Appleton*

Nevis E. (1997) *Gestalt Therapy: Perspectives and Applications* London: Gestalt Press

Nonaka I. (1994) *A Dynamic Theory of Organizational Knowledge Creation* Organization Science 5: p.14-37 (David

Baume May 2004)

O'Conner J. (2001), *NLP Workbook* London: Harper Collins

Schulz K. (2010) *Being Wrong* London: Harper Collins

Siff J. (2010) *Unlearning Meditation* Boston: Shambhala

Strasser F. and Randolph P. (2004) *Mediation: A Psychological Insight into Conflict Resolution* Continuum

Part 2: Why 'CO'–mediation

6. The challenges and advantages of co-mediating

Hanaway, Hayes, McKimm-Vorderwinkler, Mitchell, O'Kennedy, O'Hehir, Randolph, Reed

Introduction

Given that most mediators still chose to mediate alone, you may be wondering why the authors chose, whenever possible, to co-mediate. In this chapter we aim to explore what is gained by co-mediating and indeed, what the disadvantages may be.

Although many of the points are picked up in the individual chapters, this chapter will aim to present an overview of four main areas – the advantages of co-mediation, the tensions and challenges of co-mediating, the advantages of sole mediation and the challenges involved in setting up a co-mediation practice.

The advantages of co-mediation

Practical

There are many practical aspects to be considered in running a mediation. Mediators will agree a pre mediation contract with the parties, agreeing the times, venue, fees, level of confidentiality etc. Initially the tasks may be mainly administrative such as liaising with a commissioning party, collection and organisation of papers, sending out practical details to the parties, organising transportation and room bookings. The responsibility for all these elements can be shared when you are co-mediating.

Usually mediators have to put many hours into the pre-mediation phase of the work. They will contact all parties who will attend the mediation and spend time ensuring they are aware of the time and venue, and checking that this causes no problem for them. They will also take them through what mediation is and explain the process and the role of the mediator. They will begin to listen to the party's concerns and whatever they wish to tell them about the dispute. This may take place by phone or in face-to-face meetings. Having a co-mediator means that this pre-work can be done by the co-mediator who is available and thus free up the other for other work. We believe that it is vital that only one of the co-mediation partnership undertakes **all** the pre-work which is directly with the parties, as to split the work would set up the possibility of one party allaying with one of the co-mediators. One partner may concentrate on the practicalities of contracting and arranging the venue while the other makes the contact with the parties and any representatives, friends, family members, union officials or lawyers who may be attending with the parties

If the process has begun in such a way that one mediator has spoken to the parties during the pre-mediation work then it is essential that this isn't taken by the parties to indicate that this mediator is more important. To counterbalance this it is then helpful if the other mediator conducts the opening joint session, explaining the role of the mediator, the process of mediation, checking authority to settle and stressing confidentiality. This 'settling in and setting up' part of the process is very important as the parties are likely to feel anxious and in need of some reassurance. Although the process will have been explained during the pre-mediation process it helps to repeat this so that both parties hear exactly the same thing and it also allows time at the beginning were they can focus on the mediator and settle their nerves a little.

Mediation can be an exhausting process, with the majority of mediations scheduled for a day. Throughout the day, our energy levels will peak and drop. If one is working alone there is little recovery time. With a co-mediator a higher level of positive energy can be maintained by the two mediators who support each other through sharing tasks, noticing when the other is flagging and taking a more active role while they 'recover'.

Stepping out for a 'comfort break' can also be possible when we have a partner who can remain with the parties. Sometimes such a break can create a change in the dynamics. In one mediation the male mediator stepped out briefly leaving their female partner with a party who was being very negative and maintaining a very 'macho', 'I'll show them' stance towards the others in the dispute. During this brief break the party chose to show the female mediator a photograph of his young daughter and talk with some pain about his divorce. During the break between this caucus and the next the two mediators were able to consider the significance of this, noting that at some level the party wanted his caring and vulnerable side acknowledged.

Even having a partner who can pop out for extra coffee or food can be vital to the process!

The drawing up of the settlement agreement can be conducted and supervised by both mediators which we also see as a strength. Both mediators will sign to witness the agreement.

Emotional support

Mediation can at times be an emotionally draining process so to have someone to share this with can allow both co-mediators to maintain good creative energy levels throughout the mediation. Using two mediators lightens the load emotionally, they can support and 'look out' for each other, noticing and reacting to any signs of tiredness, tension or frustration perhaps arranging a break to take stock and 'refuel'.

The Harvard model, with its use of a number of individual caucus sessions with different parties, provides opportunities for co-mediators to emotionally 'off-load' between sessions – to share concerns and frustrations or air questions. It also allows the mediators to help each other remain positive at those points in the mediation where it all feels very stuck, or the intransigence of a party is proving particularly frustrating.

We can be disarmed by the way in which the content of a mediation session impacts on us emotionally. It may trigger personal memories of similar situations in our own lives and may take us back to the emotions we felt at the time, leaving us less open for offering a unique response to the party's experience of the situation they are describing. To use a psychotherapeutic term, we may 'project' our experiences onto one of the parties and may experience a response to them which is close to 'transference'. They may remind us of someone who we loved or hated in the past and we may well begin to feel similar emotional reactions towards the party. A finely tuned co-mediator will pick this up and a partnership which has established a trusting relationship will be able to openly discuss this between the caucus sessions to ensure that this does not get in the way.

The journey home from the mediation, with one's co-mediator, is an opportunity to offload any emotional aspects of the case. Having a co-mediator to share any concerns with allows the mediator to have a full sense of completion at the end of the day.

Another perspective

The mediator and co-mediator should ideally be confident enough and trust each other enough to be open to each other's (possibly different) views and perspectives. We all have different sensitivities, strengths and weaknesses. Indeed, throughout this book you will pick up that although all the authors share a belief in co-mediation the ways in which they do this vary.

If such a strong collaborative relationship exists between the co-mediators it is immensely valuable for them to use their different perspectives on the disputants' position, and for this to be expressed and explored during the mediation. Even if both co-mediators are aware of a particular point of principle for a disputant they might see it differently and so phrase a question in a different way which the party might be able to be received more easily. For this to be possible it is essential that co-mediators leave their ego at the door and accept that individual parties may response more positively to one co-mediator than to the other. It is not a competition between the two mediators but a trusting working alliance aimed at benefiting the parties.

As O'Hehir and O'Kennedy point out in their chapter, co-mediation allows for

> '*a second pair of eyes, ears and hands, which working in unison can manage and inform the mediation process with greater efficiency than a sole practitioner.*'

When the the Police take eyewitness reports of an accident, it is always interesting to see he details one witness focuses on, which is often totally absent from the reports of other witnesses. Individuals are drawn to noticing things which hold a particular significance for them personally. A mediator cannot help but bring their own interests, experiences and possible prejudices into the room. They will work hard to recognize and 'bracket' these assumptions but to have another pair of eyes on the dispute helps this process.

It may also be that there is a particular element to a case that might benefit from one working with a particular co-mediator who brings some personal, professional or cultural experience that may be relevant or reassuring to the parties. However, a mediator who feels a professional or personal connection with the parties needs to work harder at checking that he is not working from assumptions based on his own experiences and feelings and is open to the difference in the party's experience of a similar situation.

In her chapter McKimm-Vorderwinkler takes a look at the role of culture in mediation. She is clear that in her view she believes it essential to have a mediator who shares ethnicity, culture or language with the parties. Clearly there are many benefits in this, some of which are also given in Hayes chapter. However, in the wider mediation community there is some debate as to whether seeking to match a mediator's ethnic group, culture or gender to that of the client is a benefit or a hindrance. Believing there is a shared background between the mediator and the party may lead to assumptions by the mediator that similar events may have been experienced in the same way and the mediator must guard against this, taking particular care to listen carefully and explore the ways in which their own beliefs and experiences differ from those of the client, in the same way they would if they perceived little commonality with the client. It is essential that all mediators are sensitive to these issues.

Co-mediating provides the opportunity to offer a male/female partnership and partner mediators from different cultures, races and backgrounds. This can help guard against perceived 'likeness' and also against a lack of knowledge, experience or understanding of the parties' background. This can also help to model, in a very overt way, how difference can be used positively and creatively. It provides for on-the-job learning for each mediator as they hear and experience the different ways their co-mediator approaches things due their different experiences and backgrounds.

Exploring human connectedness

A co-mediating team can serve as a pathway to human connectedness in the sense that the relationship between the mediators and the relationship between the mediators and the parties can reveal the uniqueness of each individual whilst simultaneously highlighting the similarities between all individuals.

Professor Marcus Feldman of Stanford University in 2002 led research which showed that all humans are 99.9% identical and, of that tiny 0.1% difference, 94% of the variation is among individuals from the same populations and only 6% between individuals from different populations. More recent research suggests the figure is closer to 96%. However, the point is that you and I are very alike whatever our background, although the way we live our lives in this world may overtly differ considerably.

Many of the contributors to this book come from a background of existential philosophy which values the uniqueness of the individual yet recognizes a set of 'human givens' which we all share. This philosophical approach believes that inner conflict is due to an individual's confrontation with these givens of human existence. Irvin D. Yalom (1980) listed these givens as: the inevitability of death, freedom and its attendant responsibility, existential isolation and meaninglessness. In the British School of Existential therapy these givens are seen as predictable tensions and paradoxes of the four dimensions of human existence, the physical, social, personal and spiritual realms (Umwelt, Mitwelt, Eigenwelt and Uberwelt).

In co-mediation these commonalities and areas of uniqueness are explored. Through this exploration the mediators discover what is important to the party and in doing so one mediator may picks up on an important dynamic in the relationship between the parties which may be missed by their co-mediator. Through the co-mediators sharing their insights this is can then be used by both mediators to develop understanding and collaboration between the parties.

Modelling

Both co-mediators will have their every move watched by the parties. This is one reason why it is important that the mediators have a collaborative relationship which is based on trust and respect for each other's differences. Any sense of a competitive relationship cannot be hidden from the parties. Any collaborative behaviour is also clear to the parties. Indeed, whether we like it or not, the close scrutiny of the parties means that we are acting as role models.

In her chapter Hanaway focuses on the otherness of the disputants and indeed on the otherness of the co-mediator. She believes that,

> *'conflicts often ensue when we experience others as different to ourselves'.*

She posits that through the way in which co-mediators facilitate a mediation, parties can see how,

> *'...two individuals (the co-mediators) with differing worldviews can come together, using different perspectives on the dispute to create movement and creative change. The co-mediators may well see things differently from each other, they may overtly disagree but their differences are used to add richness to the resolution.'*

This may be the first time that the parties have seen two people express different perspectives and use the difference respectfully and creatively. For many, difference is perceived as threatening and the opportunity to see it modelled as positive by the co-mediators can effectively challenge that assumption.

A co-mediation team must model positive behaviour throughout the process. Mediators can demonstrate respect in simple ways, such as being punctual, reliable, honest, open and non-judgemental. They can also demonstrate effective communication by using verbal and non-verbal listening techniques such as noticing and responding to cues of discomfort or tension also by checking in with each other (and the parties) to ensure that there is a common understanding at all times.

They show respect to their co-mediator by allowing space for him to speak. If they disagree with their partner they do not try to take control, put their co-mediator down or overtly challenge their thinking. They may choose to clarify the differences in private during the break between caucuses or if the trust between the mediators is sufficiently strong they will model how to make a challenge which respects and validates the other e.g.

'That's an interesting thought, I shall think about that as I was seeing it rather differently..',

'How interesting, I had never thought of it that way...'

'Oh tell me a bit more about that way of seeing things ...'

'That's gives another perspective on things...'

'Help me understand that viewpoint ...'

They would then go on to offer it to the parties to respond... *'How does that fit with how* **you** *see things/feel about things/ have experienced/understand things...'*

Modelling such behaviour is helpful in that parties can actually see and experience it working in practice, rather than just talking about the need for people to be on time or respect, listen to each other, and reflect on the other's views. To demonstrate thoughtful and respectful challenging can provide a model for how the parties can challenge each other whilst caring for the other's self-esteem.

Although the importance of modelling has not been adequately researched, Hayes, draws our attention to the fact that

'the significance of modelling desired behaviour as a technique in effecting behaviour change is well documented in psychology literature (Bandura, 1977; Mischel, 1993)'

Value for money for the client

There are considerable benefits to the client in having two mediators, usually, for the price of one.

As long as the co-mediators have a strong collaborative relationship the financial benefits for the client are numerous. Most co-mediators do not charge the client more than they would be paying for a sole mediator.

The client has added value in having two points of contact prior and post the mediation. The client is also buying double the skills, experience, knowledge, energy and perspective and the synergy between the co-mediators which can help to generate more creative solutions.

There is also value to the client in having two styles and views and possibly mediators from different backgrounds.

Supervision

One of the great values of co-mediation is that in addition to one's own internal supervisor, we have a colleague who can help us reflect on our work throughout the day and with whom we can discuss progress, frustrations, blocks, individual prejudices and ideas. This helps to maintain a high level of neutrality and authenticity in both mediators which has a significant impact on the conflict resolution process.

In her chapter Mitchell focuses on the importance of the supervision role, acknowledging that,

> *'After I have mediated on my own I am left with a burning need to take stock and talk through my experience of the day with another mediator.'*

Our approach to mediation is a psychological one, and whilst professionals in other psychologically based professions are required to be in supervision, at present this is not required of mediators, which as Mitchell points out, is,

> *'puzzling given that mediators are caught up in relationships with their parties and have a need to talk through any concerns they may have about how they managed the mediation.'*

Throughout the mediation process we maintain rapport and trust with the parties, retain our neutrality, maintain high levels of concentration and energy, remain positive and maintain a belief that agreement is possible. These are the personal attributes we bring to mediation. Co mediation allows us to reflect on how well or poorly we are working with these attributes, providing an opportunity to discuss one's own responses with the co-mediator and thus having the potential to compensate for any lapses or shortcomings in our own responses.

We believe that this potential for 'in the moment supervision' which co-mediating provides is a real positive, particularly during the day of the mediation and in the de-briefing session. However, this is not to say that the co-mediators might not benefit from external supervision in addition in respect to good practice. It is possible that the quality of the co-mediators relationship can be such that it becomes collusive and limits the learning from the peer-supervision between the two mediators. As Reed explores in his chapter, it is as important to be open to unlearning as it is to be important to learning and a 'too comfortable' partnership may hinder this. Fresh eyes are a valuable commodity.

One role of a supervisor is to check for breaches of impartiality. A co-mediating team can carry out this check in situ and thus reduce the likelihood of mediator bias. In the preparation stage, if one mediator is aware and concerned that they may be at risk of taking sides, the other mediator can make sure that they watch out for signs and be ready to step in if the need arises. Both mediators take on this supervisory task on behalf of the other by being on guard to help prevent incidences of partiality occurring in the first place and during the feedback stage of the process can explore any incidences that have arisen to build sensitivity and alertness and capacity in remaining impartial.

When mediating alone there is a danger that the mediator is not operating as an effective internal supervisor and without the presence of another mediator this can be dangerous.

Continuing Professional Development

O'Hehir and O'Kennedy show how working with a co-mediator provides the opportunity for continuing professional development, as

> ... *we continually learn from one another. We constantly discover and rediscover each other's skills and abilities and are inspired by the insights and energy that both bring to mediation...*'

Co-mediators often travel to and from the mediations together. This presents the opportunity to learn from each other what each is taking from the mediation in terms of their own development.

Having a co-mediator present ensures that standards do not slip. We are aware that our partner sees our skills and knowledge and in a trusting partnership any difficulties encountered can be reflected on and analysed as an opportunity for further learning and growth. We learn through working with, watching and listening to our co-mediator during the mediations as much as we do through the shared reflections at the de-briefing.

On a practical level co-mediating partners can share knowledge of upcoming conferences, training, journals and books, can share and disseminate their reading and meet to reflect and share on any CPD opportunities they have undertaken.

b) The tensions and challenges of co-mediating,

Trust

As we have seen, co-mediating calls for a high level of trust in one's co-mediator. Our skills, strengths and weaknesses will be exposed to another professional. We need to ensure that we feel able to accept their praise and their constructive criticism openly.

If we encounter a case where we recognize a potential bias in ourself we need to trust our co-mediator enough to be able to share this with them at the outset and call on them to help monitor how effective I am in not bringing the bias to play in the mediation.

Choosing the wrong co-mediator

To find oneself working with a co-mediator who we do not trust can make the process a very uncomfortable one. This is more likely to happen when the decision has been taken for both mediators to hold the same level of responsibility in the process.

It is essential that one is clear with any potential co-mediator about our own respective values/principles regarding mediation. There are many mediation-training organizations and not all share the same ethos. Some training focuses most strongly on the psychological aspects of conflict whereas others focus more on the process and structure. In order to trust one's partner and form a strong working alliance there needs to be a shared understanding of the reasons why conflict resolution is important to them.

One also needs to agree with a co-mediator the ways in which constructive criticism can be made. When is it appropriate? ... during the breaks between caucuses? ... at the end of the mediation? Or at some other agreed time?

A deep understanding of power dynamics is required of partners in co-mediation. A mediator who does not understand this will be a 'wrong' mediator in any co-mediating agreement. Co-mediators have to be very aware of how they individually use their power, both in relation to each other and to the parties. A mediator who wishes to take centre stage is unlikely to be a good solo mediator and will certainly make a poor co-mediator.

Co-mediators must also be very sensitive about their own need for self-esteem and that need in their partner. It is necessary to show respect to one's partner at all times, particularly at times of disagreement as co-mediators model ways of dealing with disagreements. It is essential never to 'put down' one's partner and to know how to pick up cues as to where and when your input is needed and when it isn't. There is no room for vying for centre stage in a co-mediation partnership. The needs of the parties are most important and may require one mediator to be in the forefront whilst the other takes a more supportive and less obvious role. Any competitive elements between the two co-mediators could prove disastrous to the success of the process.

We have already stressed the importance of human connectedness and although co-mediation more overtly demonstrates any negative dynamics between the co-mediators it would be wrong to consider that it is absent in the sole mediator model. Indeed the presence of a second mediator can help prevent this being played out by the mediator in relation to their interaction with the parties and the parties' interaction with each other.

Danger of Manipulation

It is a natural response for most human beings to have a desire to be liked and to want the mediator to see them as being in the right and the other party as being wrong. It is not unknown for a party to try to get a mediator to like them and dislike the other party. This happens with sole mediators and in co-mediation.

One of the dangers of a co-mediating model in which the co-mediators separate is the potential for the parties to attempt to engage in manipulative behaviour with the co-mediators and attempt set them against each other. A good skilled and experienced mediator will be very aware of this and work to avoid it.

However, this can happen from the outset where one mediator may have taken responsibility to undertake all the pre-mediation work. This means that the parties and the mediator will have formed some impression of each other and begun to form some kind of working relationship. At this stage this may be either positive or negative.

Even when the mediator is careful not to agree or disagree with the parties it is possible that one party may try to make a mediator appear impartial e.g. *'Your colleague agreed with me that...'*, *'That's not what your co-mediator has been saying...'* etc. This may still happen even though it is clear that a mediator would not collude with any party in this way. Clearly impartiality in the mediator lies at the heart of the mediation process.

For this reason, mediators working with the Harvard model, in which there may be a large number of private caucuses, believe that the co-mediators should remain together throughout the process. Very conscious of confidentiality and the importance of how easily words can be misinterpreted they will attempt not to become messengers for the parties, only taking across offers or other communication which has been rigorous checked out with the party and where the party has given explicit permission for it to be shared with the other party. The mediators will only bring the parties together in a joint session when they believe a commonality and a way forward has been identified they will then ideally look to the parties to express their needs and for the parties themselves to disclose information to the other party at the joint sessions. This means that both mediators will go to see one party in each of the private caucuses and then both go to see the other party in all their private caucuses. It can be tempting when pushed for time to try to split the mediators but this increases the danger of things being misinterpreted or manipulated and mediators must work with this in mind.

Other mediation models do not follow the same process and may rarely, if at all, hold private caucuses. The co-mediators will plan in the opening joint meeting which mediator will work with which party in the event of a caucus meeting. Following a caucus meeting the whole group resumes, with the mediators spending a couple of moments agreeing how they will share what was discussed in the caucus to the benefit of the meeting.

All mediators have a duty to work with unhelpful behaviour from the parties as it arises, to explore its cause and seek to understand what the party is trying to achieve through these words and/or actions. No action or statement is without meaning.

Communication

Some mediators only co-mediate with the same partner all of the time. Others will co-mediate with a number of different partners. Whatever the arrangement, the way the two communicate together has to thought about and carefully carried out.

The mode of communication is seen by the parties and provides a model of how to communicate with another person, even when the views held differ. Co-mediators need to have a very respectful way of communicating, particularly when they are in disagreement. They also need to know when to speak and when to leave a silence for their co-mediator.

This does not mean that the co-mediators are clones of each other. In respecting differences they may have very different communication styles. One co-mediator's language and style may be more informal than the other's, one may hold relevant technical knowledge and language which the other does not, these differences allows the party a choice of styles in which they may feel comfortable expressing themselves.

Ego

A danger in co-mediating is that the ego of one or both co-mediators gets in the way. We have already alluded to the fact that sometimes a co-mediator's personality, experience or style makes it easier for them to set up a trusting working alliance with one or both parties. Their co-mediator needs to greet this positively and not feel threatened by it. It is not a reflection of them; it is just natural that we get on with some people more quickly than we do with others. A mediator who is looking to gain glory or affirmation from being a mediator or seeks to 'rescue' a situation or 'drive through' a resolution may not find what they are looking for in a co-mediation approach.

A co-mediator has to learn to step back when their partner is making progress and to resist the temptation to say something just in order to justify their presence and boost their ego.

Financial

Although there is a financial advantage to the client in co-mediation, there is a financial disadvantage for a mediator who chooses to co-mediate.

Co-mediators who work as equal partners usually split the fee 50/50 and do not charge the client extra for the involvement of two mediators rather than one. Clearly this means they are earning half the fee they would if mediating alone.

In other models where there is a lead mediator and an assistant mediator the fee is split differently with the usual arrangement being that the lead mediator takes most of the fee. In some cases a lead mediator will take the entire fee and expect an assistant to work pro bono.

Novice mediators looking to co-mediate in order to gain experience may find that not only are they not paid but also that they have to fund their own expenses.

c) The advantages of sole mediation

Most of the advantages of mediating alone are more or less the opposite of those for co-mediating.

Financially there is a gain, as the fee does not have to be split two ways.

The extra dynamic of working sensitively with another, in order to model good communication and power dynamics, is not present in sole mediation and so there is less to take the mediator's attention away from the parties.

As a sole mediator you are still open to the potentiality of parties' being manipulative but do not have to worry about them trying to set you up against your co-mediator.

It may feel better for one's ego to be the one entirely 'in charge' of the process.

d) Setting up a co-mediation practice.

In setting up a co-mediation practice one has to consider carefully how compatible one is with one's co-mediator(s). There are also a number of questions which partners must address in establishing their practice.

Sharing philosophy

Do you always wish to work with the same person or do you

wish to build a pool of potential co-mediators who will be members or affiliates within the practice? Both models have the potential to work well but need to be considered differently.

However, as stated earlier all those in a partnership must share the same understanding of what conflict is and what it means to mediate. People change and so regular opportunities to check that all members of the practice continue to share the same approach need to be built in.

Understanding the other

How can we build understanding of each other across the practice?

Working with the same mediator allows both members of the partnership to understand each other's style and to know each other's strengths and weaknesses. Through the regularity of the work one comes to understand what kinds of things challenge your partner and in what areas they hold specialist skills and knowledge.

This is also true where there is a team of like-minded mediators who form a practice in which they may co-mediate with any other member of the team.

Flexibility

The nature of mediation work is that it is unpredictable and so requires both mediators to be open minded and flexible as well as being clear and open in their communication.

How can be help to develop flexibility in our pratice?

We need a co-mediator who we trust will know when to take the lead and when to be a follower. We can agree certain signs meaning *'Take over'* or *'Leave this to me'* or even *'Help, I'm a mediator get me out of here!'*

When working with a new co-mediator the new partners must put work and energy into forming that level of understanding.

Role and Financial issues

How can we ensure clarify about every partners' roles?

It is important in a partnership agreement that everyone is clear about the nature of the partnership.

Is it a partnership in which the roles are equal or is there a lead mediator?

How will the fees be split?

If one partner does all the setting up and takes part in the mediation do they get more than the partner who is only involved in the actual mediation?

What happens when one partner takes the lead and the other is designated 'assistant'? Answers to all these questions must be clear from the outset.

There is a lot of practical administration in setting up a mediation. There needs to be clarity about which co-mediator is taking on what role or there is a danger of something being missed. These roles may shift for each mediation but clarity is essential.

All these issues need to be clearly spelt out in drawing up an agreement to work as a co-mediator.

CPD

There are questions in this area too.

What supervision and continual professional development do the partners commit too?

Do they need to do the same courses so they can reflect on them together or can they divide what to attend so that they can cascade the learning?

What requirement does the practice hold regarding supervision?

Much of the above is discussed in the form of questions because there are no right answers. What is essential is that these are discussed and the co-mediators are clear about what is required of them in the co-mediation practice. This may need to be written down in the form of an agreed contract.

Miscellaneous

Just as in setting up any practice, consideration has to be given to practical matters such as ensuring the correct level of professional indemnity insurance for all partners.

Decisions have to be taken about the nature of the practice or company that it being set up. Given the focus of this book it isn't appropriate to go into detail here but it does need careful consideration.

Conclusion

We would encourage all mediators to explore the benefits and challenges of co-mediation. Co-mediation has a flow and dynamic to it which can be magical and inspire and support positive outcomes for those in dispute.

It continually challenges the co-mediators to provide high quality mediation whilst supporting them in that pursuit.

Despite these challenges we believe that the benefits to the parties and to the mediators far outweigh any perceived disadvantages.

References

Yalom I. D. (1980) *'Existential Psychotherapy'*; Basic Books

Cooper M. (2003) *'Existential Therapies'* Sage Publications

Part 3: Different co-mediation models

7. Different co-mediation approaches

Monica Hanaway

There are many differences in the ways that people chose to co-mediate. The contributors in this book, although all using a psychological approach, have different preferences with regard to the co-mediating models they use. Most have experienced more than one approach.

Perhaps the most democratic approach is when both mediators are given equality in the mediation process. There is no lead mediator. The way this works has to be very clearly thought about and agreed by the co-mediators. Any lack of clarify could lead to conflict between them. It is a model which requires a great deal of trust in one's co-mediator, a set of shared values, good ego strength and the energy to fully engage with the flow of the mediation. It is the co-mediating model which I use most often and so I shall briefly describe how I employ this model.

Equal mediators

When our company is commissioned to undertake a mediation, the two mediators to work with the case will be identified from our network of affiliated mediators. An information leaflet is then sent out to those involved in the dispute. This explains the mediation process and introduces the individuals who will be co-mediating by name, giving a little information about their background. Wherever possible this includes photographs of the mediators so that when the parties arrive at the venue they can name and identify their mediators.

One mediator then takes on the pre-mediation work. This consists of making the initial phone contact with all the different parties in the dispute and allowing them the opportunity to speak in confidence about their views on the dispute and any concerns they may have about the mediation process. In this model it is important, that no matter the number of disputants, this task is not split between the two mediators as this could set up the possibility of manipulation and a belief that one mediator 'belonged to' and may favour the party with whom she had spoken.

The other mediator may well spend time on the more practical aspects of the mediation, agreeing the venue, organising the travel, getting the pre-mediation contract in place etc.

On the day of the mediation the parties may start by feeling more comfortable with the mediator they have already had telephone contact with. For this reason that mediator takes a more subdued role at the start of the mediation, allowing their co-mediator to deal with the introductions, explain the process, emphasis confidentiality, check people have the authority to settle and generally be seen as equally important in the mediation.

During the mediation itself each mediator is sensitive to the ways in which the client works with each mediator. If the client seems more comfortable with one mediator then that mediator will probably take a more prominent role with that client. However, it is important the both mediators are active and each allows for interventions from the other, thus modeling collaborative working.

Lead Mediators

In other models, one of the mediators takes the lead role, whilst the other assists. One mediator may be more experienced and therefore takes on a mentoring role in relation to their co-mediator. The extent to which the mentee is active in the mediation will differ greatly between partnerships. Some experienced mediators may require their co-mediator to be silent unless invited by them to contribute, other may give the mentee an assistant role, ensuring the safety and comfort of everyone or taking any notes which may be required, others will encourage the mentee to contribute to the process.

Even when both mediators are experienced model using a lead mediator may be preferred. In some instances one mediator may have a particular expertise in the area of the dispute and may focus on that whilst the co-mediator takes particular note of the interpersonal dynamics. The criteria for deciding who takes the lead role will vary according to the needs of each mediation and the needs or expectations of the client.

In other mediations where the language of one or more of the disputants is different from the lead mediators, the lead mediators may be an experienced mediator and the co-mediator an individual who understands the mediation process but is acting as an interpreter.

For some disputes the gender, race or culture of the mediator may be considered very important by one of the disputants. In these cases the lead mediator may have been chosen because they belong to one of these categories whilst it is less important in the case of their co-mediator.

As we can see there are several different models. There is no 'correct' model. It is important that the needs of the parties are at the forefront of any decision about who should 'lead'. The next chapters will look a little more closely on some of the models.

8. Co-Mediating with Novice Mediators

Paul Randolph

Introduction

As Course Director of the mediation training course at the School of Psychotherapy and Counselling Psychology at Regent's College, London, I am regularly asked by graduates of the course to provide opportunities for them to gain mediation experience through co-mediating with me. These graduates come from a very wide variety of backgrounds and so bring with them particular 'conditioned' approaches some of which can be very different from those embraced by the mediator. This chapter explores the challenges and the benefits that such experiences can provide, both to the mediator and to the novice or apprentice co-mediator – as well as to the parties.

The demand for co-mediation

The mediation 'profession' remains, as yet, almost wholly unregulated. Anyone can place a plaque outside their door proclaiming themselves to be a mediator: they need have no experience – nor even any qualification or training.

However, the most common route towards gainful employment for a newly-qualified mediator is to join one of the 60 or more Mediation Provider Panels to be found around the country. These panels are invariable 'accredited' by the Civil Mediation Council ("CMC"), and this accreditation in turn involves some degree of regulation. Section E of the Guidance Notes to the 2011 Civil Mediation Council Provider Accreditation Scheme reads as follows:

"(1) An Accredited Mediation Provider must require its new mediators to have observed at least three civil or commercial mediations over the last 12 months before they are eligible for appointment as a lead mediator. One of these observerships may be of a role-play nature.

(2)   All the Provider's mediators must have observed or conducted at least two civil or commercial mediations in the 12 months prior to its accreditation (or re-accreditation) in order to ensure that they have current practice experience."

These provisions, together with the very natural desire to gain as much valuable experience as possible before launching onto an unsuspecting market, create a significant demand for co-mediation or 'observership' opportunities and experience.

It is also my firm view that there is a corresponding duty – whether moral, ethical or professional – upon all mediators to offer novice mediators every opportunity to secure that requisite experience. As a member of the Bar, I shared a similar moral and professional duty to take on a 'pupil barrister' as soon as I was eligible to do so. These 'pupillage' opportunities were vital in providing the young novice barrister a good start in their career at the Bar.

And so it is with co-mediation 'apprenticeships'. They provide a highly valuable – and valued – chance to share knowledge and experience, as well as creating (hopefully) a standard of mediating to which the novice mediator can aspire. At the same time it helps to lift that cloud of mystique which hangs over all graduates from mediation courses: they yearn to see the 'real thing' after spending many hours in the heavily artificial environment of the 'mock mediation case study'. These co-mediation opportunities help to move graduates seamlessly from the academic environment of a mediation course into the real or commercial world of mediated disputes.

Reluctance to take an assistant

There regrettably appears to be a widespread reluctance amongst experienced mediators to have or take with them a novice or assistant mediator. The explanations – or are they excuses? – are legion: "the assistants only get in the way"; "they add nothing to the process and simply irritate"; "the parties don't like it when you bring someone else to the mediation"; "it's just another person in the room to worry about"; "the parties won't pay for an assistant or co-mediator, so that means I am expected to pay them a fee myself".

I would venture to suggest that the true reason is not attractive or flattering to the mediation fraternity. Many mediators tend to revert to old – and bad – habits after a period of time without further training or 'refresher' courses. A very eminent former Court of Appeal Judge, an alumnus of the Regent's College course, returned for a one-day 'Refresher' at the College. As an experienced mediator, he candidly expressed surprise at the fact that others on the Refresher, who were there because they had not gained their accreditation first time around, seemed to display skills of a higher standard than those who were there simply 'to refresh'. The more experienced the mediator the greater is the likely period that will have elapsed since their original training. Consequently the highly experienced (and much sought-after) mediators can be some of the worst culprits. Some will have a sufficient degree of self-awareness to acknowledge that they may not be deploying the skills in the manner in which they were first taught. They may even be aware that they have a tendency to "cut corners". Others may have a sneaking suspicion that, were they to be observed by another mediator, fresh out of a training course, they might be seen as having joined the cohorts of "trashers and bashers" – those who 'trash' each side's case so as to lower their expectations, and then 'bash' heads together to compel them to reach a settlement.

In my view, it is this very fear of being observed and possibly shown up to be wanting, which is the cause of so much reluctance to use a co-mediator. This fear is one of the issues that a novice mediator must bear in mind when acting as an assistant to an experienced mediator. On the other hand, one of the principal benefits of having an assistant mediator is that this provides an effective mechanism for the more experienced mediator to receive constructive feedback from another mediator 'fresh out of school'. Both of these aspects are examined in greater detail below.

The role of the lead mediator in co-mediation

The lead mediator, for the purposes of this Chapter, is assumed to be the one with significantly more experience than that of the assistant or co-mediator. The lead mediator must therefore take control of the relationship at the outset, so as to avoid confusion, embarrassment, hesitancy and doubt, which might otherwise permeate throughout the process.

The first obligation on the part of the lead mediator is to secure the permission or consent of both parties to the presence of an assistant. There can be little more embarrassing for a novice assistant than to arrive and discover that he or she is neither expected nor wanted. To be introduced to the party at the commencement of the mediation and to hear: "What is he/she doing here? We did not agree to his/her attendance!" can be extremely disconcerting, and not an ideal way to begin a career as a mediator.

Generally, the parties will not be expected to pay for an assistant mediator, especially if he or she is a "mere novice". Consequently they will not be expecting an assistant to be there unless they have been specifically so told. There will rarely be any significant objection to an assistant, especially if some brief CV or biographical note has been furnished to both parties, possibly showing some element of relevance in their presence.

Similarly if the lead mediator has not established or made clear to the assistant the exact nature, extent and boundaries of his or her part in the process, it will greatly detract both from the learning process and from any assistance that the co-mediator might be able to provide to the lead mediator.

It is of course vital that the mediator be wholly clear and unambiguous in the instructions and explanation given to the novice mediator. This can perhaps be illustrated by the following experience.

I had invited a young novice mediator to accompany me at a commercial mediation, and noticed that she was reticently hanging back when I went to speak to one of the parties. I took her to one side and explained to her that "we are a team – where I go, you go". A few minutes later, she promptly followed me into the 'Gents' toilet!

The lead mediator should therefore give considerable thought to the type of relationship and the nature of the interaction he or she wishes to create during their collaboration. This will naturally depend upon a number of factors:

- the level of experience, if any, of the co-mediator

- any significant difference in age between lead mediator and co-mediator

- ethnic and gender considerations

- professional background of both lead and co-mediators

For example, my communications and dealings when co-mediating with a retired Judge were entirely different to those when I was with a young psychotherapist. The psychotherapist felt she should adopt a role more akin to an observer than a 'co-mediator': her sense of "complete inexperience" made that seem more appropriate; whereas the retired Judge found great difficulty in to relinquishing his usual element of control, and almost instinctively wished to take a more active part.

In such circumstances, however, lead mediators need to apply the very same techniques and skills as they would with the parties: they must consider the 'safety' and comfort of the assistant mediator just as much as they would that of the parties in the dispute. The assistant will be just as uncertain, just as nervous, and equally desirous of making a good impression upon the mediator, as the parties. The lead mediator therefore needs to be empathic and non-judgmental, so as to avoid making the assistant feel uncomfortable, put down, or embarrassed in any way. Just as in training, the self-esteem of the assistant mediator should be addressed: it should not be rendered lower at the end of the mediation than when the assistant first walked in.

The lead mediator, as the term suggests, should thus take the lead when a novice is assisting. As stated above, he or she will need to define clearly their respective roles, and will need to ensure that the assistant has fully understood the implications of what is expected of him or her.

Some lead mediators will prefer their assistants to do very little in terms of mediating, but more in terms of securing the comfort and well-being of the parties (see *further below*). Others will treat their assistant as precisely that – someone to assist them in all aspects of the mediation, perhaps on a more equal footing. This may include being the 'scribe' in the use of flip-charts, – and asking the occasional pertinent question. Whenever I use an assistant who has been trained at the SPCP at Regent's College, I am usually confident that he or she will always ask any such questions in the most tentative manner, so as to allow the party the space to disagree or refute the question without embarrassment or irritation.

Most importantly, however, the lead mediator will expect the assistant to be a valuable extra pair of eyes and ears. This is dealt with further under *The Role of the Assistant*. During the mediation, the lead mediator should ideally – always, if appropriate, initiate a brief chat with the assistant, after each session, whether a joint session with all parties or a private session with one of the parties alone. These chats are vital for the lead mediator to 'bounce off' the assistant any ideas, views, perceptions, feelings and emotions gleaned or created in the immediately preceding session. Equally, if not more importantly, it provides an opportunity for the assistant mediator to furnish the lead mediator with the benefit of their own observations, perceptions and intuitions. Lead mediators should not be reticent in asking their assistants for their views in these instances: the assistant will invariably have seen and noted matters which the lead mediator may have missed, and furnishing these observations will normally be much appreciated by the mediator.

In the later stages of the mediation, once offers, proposals, counter-offers and formulae for settlement are being canvassed by both parties, the mediation process inevitably becomes more strategic. This is where mediators need to consider carefully how best to move matters forward towards settlement. This may involve considerations of how to deliver messages they have been asked to 'take across', taking into account whether the message contains 'good news' or bad, and whether it is palatable or unpalatable. In my view, it is firmly part of the mediator's role to frame, and if necessary re-frame, such messages before delivery. This is where the assistant can be most helpful. Contributing to the discussion with the mediator and helping him or her decide what next steps to take, and how best to take them, can be a most constructive and beneficial exercise of the assistant's role. Conversations might take place around the following questions:

- *"Now that we have gleaned this information from one of the parties, what are we to do with it?"*

- *"How are we to put this information to best use?"*

- *"What do you think their reaction will be when we put this to the other party?"*

- *"How can we deliver this message in the best possible light?"*

- *"How do we put this to the other party in a way that will avoid a walk-out by them?"*

The process whereby the lead mediator consults with the assistant and 'chews over' some of these questions and issues between sessions with each party, can not only be useful, but furnishes the assistant with enormous self-confidence: the assistant can feel included, useful, and pleased perhaps to be deferred to by the lead mediator for an opinion.

The Role of the Assistant Mediator

Many lead mediators will readily initiate the discussion as to their respective roles, and what is or is not expected of the assistant. But if they do not, the assistant may need to be pro-active in pinning down the lead mediator properly to define their respective roles. There is little wrong in the assistant contacting the lead mediator and asking: "Can we meet for a quick chat before the mediation, so that I can understand exactly what you will expect of me during the day?" If such a question leads to perceptible irritation, it may perhaps be time to find another co-mediation elsewhere! Or alternatively, go along for the experience – and be prepared at the end to make a list of issues which you would have handled differently!

The role and duties expected of the assistant will vary from one mediator to another. Some lead mediators will be wary of any significant involvement by the assistant in the mediation; and will want the assistant to restrict their role to more of a 'domestic' nature. This may include meeting and greeting the parties, showing them to their respective rooms, ensuring that they have proper heating and ventilation, adequate supplies of coffee, tea, water and biscuits, and that they are aware of the location of the toilets!

If this is the full extent of the role as delineated by the lead mediator, the assistant should not despair. Remember that the mediator – like all the parties – comes into the process with the same uncertainties, doubts and concerns – and with the same issues of self-esteem to protect and maintain.

- *"Will I be successful today?"*

- *"Will I be able to establish rapport with the parties?"*

- *"What if they don't like me?"*

- *"What if I lose my temper with one or other of the parties?"*

- *"What if the assistant does not like me or my approach?"*

- *"What if the assistant thinks I am a poor mediator?"*

These fears illustrate a basic and obvious truth: the mediator has similar issues with self-esteem is everybody else in the mediation room. The mediator will have a need to protect and reinforce his or her own self-esteem just as all others in the process. Consequently, the assistant may need to use the very same techniques taught on the course in his or her interactions with the lead mediator. Asking the mediator in all innocence: "Why did you put that question to the party at that particular point?" may be perceived and received by the mediator as 'judgmental' or a criticism – requiring him or her to explain, defend and justify the actions to the assistant.

So the assistant's role may need to be a sensitive one, ensuring that the mediator does not feel his or her toes are trodden upon, or worse still, that he or she has been 'usurped' in the role as lead mediator.

But what does a novice assistant do if he or she does not agree with the approach or manner adopted by the lead mediator? What if there is a fundamental difference in the way the mediator handles the process in comparison with what was taught to the assistant? I remember when as a novice assistant, I was astonished to be asked by a very senior and experienced mediator on the evening prior to the mediation: "So, Paul, what position do you think we should try to get the parties to reach by the end of tomorrow?" My astonishment was driven by the training I had had, namely to the effect that the mediator should not enter the mediation process with any agenda of their own. The concept of working out in advance to where the parties might be led –or pushed – by the mediator was anathema to all that I had been taught – and which I now teach.

Whatever the situation, the assistant mediator should at all costs seek to avoid alienating the lead mediator. To irritate, offend, or undermine the lead mediator would do little to enhance the learning process of the co-mediation relationship, and might also adversely interfere with the mediation process itself. Rather the assistant mediator should, at the appropriate time, endeavour to secure from the mediator the rationale or thinking behind, and motivation for, any actions or methodological approaches adopted by the lead mediator. In so doing the assistant mediator will no doubt use the very same techniques as, hopefully, they will have been taught on their training course: open, non-judgemental questions, paraphrasing and reflecting back, In many instances the assistant mediator is given an opportunity to furnish written feed-back to the mediation provider setting out his or her views as to the manner in which the lead mediator conducted the mediation. This may be the most appropriate forum for making any criticisms or comments, however harsh, that the assistant mediator feels duty bound to make.

On the positive side, and as stated above, the principal asset in the role of the assistant is to be a valuable extra pair of eyes and ears for the mediator. This is particularly pertinent in the joint session, when invariably the mediator's eye-contact will be primarily with the party speaking. Here, the assistant mediator will be able to see and assess the reactions of the other parties around the table. Such observations will complement the picture that the lead mediator gathers as to the dynamics in the room and the differing emotional drivers of the issues in the dispute.

A further important and beneficial function that the assistant mediator can bring to the mediation is to act as a foil to the lead mediator if and when circumstances demand it. For example, should the lead mediator become visibly irritated or impatient with any of the parties, the assistant can usefully interpose by making a more palliative intervention. There have been many occasions when I have been rescued by an assistant mediator after making an utterance which, from the moment it left my mouth, I felt was clearly inappropriate, and led to an adverse reaction on the part of those to whom I was speaking. The assistant mediator, noticing what had taken place, was able to interject with a softer and more empathic question, thereby deflecting the perhaps unfortunate effect of my own words.

By remaining slightly distant from the main interaction between the lead mediator and the parties the assistant mediator is better able to observe the different reactions of the parties and to pick up the more subtle nuances of what is going on in the room. I have often compared this to a club tennis player sitting in the pavilion watching other players on court and being bewildered at the nature and extent of apparently simple mistakes made by experienced players on court – only to make those very same simple crass errors myself when I got on the court. When the assistant is merely observing, he or she can pick up an enormous amount of highly valuable additional emotional information. This by remaining "a semi-detached participant" in the process, yet being fully attentive at all times, the assistant mediator is able fully to complement the lead mediator in many aspects of his role.

Other Benefits for the Lead Mediator

In addition to the stated benefits of an extra pair of eyes and ears, the contributions of an assistant mediator can be constructive in several other ways. The ability to discuss and evaluate with the assistant mediator the progress made at each stage of the mediation, whether through joint sessions or private sessions, should not be underestimated. A differing perspective, voiced by the assistant mediator, can shed an entirely different light upon the lead mediator's view of the issues and can lead to different and more productive avenues being explored in the private sessions. The eagerness of the mediator can be tempered by the assistant, while at other times the mediator's despondency may equally be lifted.

Feedback given by the assistant mediator to the mediator, both during and after the mediation, is an important aspect of co-mediation. Even though the lead mediator is conscious of having to perform well for the benefit of the parties, their legal advisers and others, the presence of an assistant mediator who is carefully observing and noting the lead mediator's every move and word, creates an added dimension to that mediator's conduct. Any feedback that the parties or their lawyers give, whether formally or informally, following the conclusion of the mediation may never be as pertinent as that given by a freshly trained assistant. Experienced mediators need the confines of an observed environment so as to avoid lapsing into those all too easy bad habits and shortcuts. As has been stated on mediation courses many times, the mediator's skills are counter-intuitive: they have to be learned and layered over unlearned sand previously conditioned behaviour. With the passage of time and the stresses of many mediations under their belt, the experienced mediators can all too easily 'revert to type', adopting yet again all those conditioned reflexes and traits that were so carefully drummed out of them during training. The novice mediators will be only too aware of these behaviours taking place when they see it in front of them during the mediation. Feedback to that effect will therefore be most salutary, and is a most effective way of maintaining even an experienced mediator's standards and techniques at a high level.

Other benefits for the Assistant Mediator

The novice mediator will inevitably emerge from a training course evangelistic and eager to see the 'real thing'. The mock mediations will have been entertaining and informative but will have only served to wet their appetite for observing a real dispute with real parties and a 'real mediator.' They will almost certainly believe that the real thing is very different to the mock mediations on the course. In this they are likely to be surprised and may even be disappointed. The magic of mediation is that it is an almost natural and imperceptible process – despite the skills used being counter-intuitive. The mediation tends to unfold chronologically: the parties set out their stalls in their opening statements in the joint session and the mediator does nothing other than listen. The parties separate into private session and again the mediator does little other than listen. The reflecting back, paraphrasing and summarising, if done well, become an almost indiscernible and undetectable part of natural conversation. I often feel almost fraudulent vis-à-vis the assistant mediator in the early parts of the mediation: I am concerned they will not be learning very much from me as I am doing very little in the mediation. It is only in the later more strategic stages of the process, when the acute – and sometimes desperate – negotiations take place that I feel I begin to earn my fee.

Inappropriate interventions by the assistant

One of the beauties of mediation is the informality of the process. The proceedings are not being recorded verbatim, nor are the words and phrases used being "taken down and used in evidence". Consequently things said and words used can be retracted. There may be many occasions when both the experienced mediator and the novice assistant realise that what they have just said or asked was inappropriate – or even plain wrong. To acknowledge this, and possibly apologise, will not only serve to rectify the situation but may also enhance the rapport and trust between the parties and the mediator. "I'm sorry, that came out quite wrong..." or "Sorry, I did not mean it to sound like that..." can serve to build an even stronger bridge in the relationship. By so doing, the mediator demonstrates his or her fallibility, and manifests an acceptance that 'we may not all be perfect'. Consequently, the novice assistant should not feel devastated if he or she makes a 'faux pas' in such circumstances. It is easily corrected, and assistants should take the courage to do so themselves, either as soon as possible, or even much later: it may matter little when the correction is made, but it might cause damage if it is not done at all. It should be an overriding principle for the assistant that all or any errors, or inappropriate or inadvertent utterances or a faux pas be addressed, rather than swept under the carpet in the hope that 'nobody noticed'.

The lead mediator should also seek to smooth over any feathers possibly ruffled by the novice assistant. Whether and how to do this should be openly discussed in the intervals between private sessions, and the assistant should have no qualms about saying: "I feel very silly about having said or done that ... Can we rectify it in some way?"

The Benefits to the Parties

Finally, what about the parties? Do they derive any benefit from the presence of a novice assistant? The parties are undeniably "getting two for the price of one", but is it helpful to them to know that they are being carefully observed at all times? Do they relish the thought that their positions and their discussions with the mediator are being dissected and analysed by the two mediators when they leave the room?

The lead mediator will need to be sensitive to such possible concerns, and address them either in the pre-mediation contact, or in the opening joint session. A careful outline to the parties of the role and purpose of the assistant will help to alleviate any apprehension or disquiet on their part.

The parties should appreciate the added attention given to them – even if it is only in respect of their physical comfort in the rooms. The consideration that the assistant can give to the heating and ventilation, to the continuous supply of fresh coffee and tea, can be a much welcomed 'added value'. It also enables the lead mediator to concentrate on the issue of building trust and rapport in more direct and pertinent ways.

Parties can occasionally turn to the assistant for added support. They will invariably spend considerable time and much effort in trying to 'get the mediator 'on side', and in circumstances where they might feel the mediator is not sufficiently 'with them', they may seek to draw in the assistant, to seek to persuade him or her of the strength of their case. This can create difficulties: the assistant will wish to avoid – and should avoid – undermining the lead med any way. It would be understandable for the assistant to appear reluctant to respond to the parties for fear of appearing to differ in approach or level of empathy. Yet, at the same time, for the assistant it is an opportunity almost too good to miss: to further build that so important trusting relationship with the parties. 'Empathy and acceptance' will be the key, and the assistant can do no harm to either the lead mediator or the parties if he or she simply empathises with the parties' position. As empathy properly conveyed should not signify agreement or approval, it will not interfere with the lead mediator's approach – even if he or she is deep into reality testing!

Conclusion

The parties will ultimately benefit from having two people giving them their undivided attention. This may be the most important aspect of co-mediation in general: the parties can be made to feel that they are being truly heard, not just by one mediator but by two. Through the occasional sensitive intervention by the novice assistant, with the proper use of all the techniques and skills of active listening recently acquired, by the occasional paraphrase or summary, the assistant can support, complement and enhance the lead mediator's function and role throughout mediation.

9. Co-Mediating with an Established Partner : The Amicus Model

Mary Lou O'Kennedy and Phil O'Hehir

Introduction

This chapter describes the Amicus Private Practice Co-Mediation Model used in our mediation work with corporate, professional and private clients. It is a model which is informed by our individual training and adapted by our experience in the field over the past five years. We both initially experienced co-mediation in our community mediation training and pro bono community mediation work. We have since adapted the community mediation model in our private commercial practice within our company, Amicus Mediation Ltd. Our belief in the benefits of co-mediation comes from this practical application in commercial, workplace, family and community mediations and the successful positive outcomes we have seen.

It is our hope that we will inspire others to consider co-mediation in their work and stimulate discussion of its benefits, methods and practice. We are working on the assumption that the reader has a basic working knowledge of the mediation process. Thus we will emphasise and focus on those aspects peculiar to co-mediation as distinct from mediation as a sole practitioner.

We will first outline and discuss our definition of co-mediation and associated terms which we use throughout the chapter, we will then highlight the different tasks which the mediators must manage in mediation and describe how the Amicus Private Practice Co-mediation Model addresses each one. We will provide examples of our experience in the field to illustrate how the Amicus Private Practice Model operates.

Concepts and Definitions

The Amicus definition of *'co-mediation'* is one which we have developed and defined in the following way:

> *'Co-mediation is a process in which two neutral third parties work in partnership to facilitate those involved in a dispute to communicate effectively with one another and reach their own agreement.'*

In this context we define *'partnership'* as

> *'A working relationship between two mediators involving close cooperation between them having pre-specified and agreed roles, responsibilities and equal status'*

At the outset of mediation we will have agreed our separate roles and responsibilities. It is accepted between us however that each of us is free to determine the level of our own input during the mediation and that we have mutual respect for each other's judgement and opinion as the mediation develops. The co-mediation model which we practice is one which recognises the equal status of both mediators in terms of their interventions, perceptions and opinions.

David Richbell defines co-mediation in the following way;

> *'Co-mediation is the harmonious working of two complementary mediators who offer a diversity of skills, experience and personality.' (Newmark C. and Monaghan A., 2005)*

The aspects of harmony and complementarities between the mediators are also important concepts which underpin the value which the co-mediation process brings to disputing parties. There must be a sense of harmony and mutual regard between the mediators. It is the demonstration of this harmony between both parties which will generate a spirit of harmony into the mediation, encouraging a positive working atmosphere and ultimately agreement between the parties. According to Bowling and Hoffman ' *when we are feeling at peace with ourselves and the world around us, we are better able to bring peace into the room*' (Bowling D. and Hoffman D., 2003, pg 14). In our experience it also holds true that there must be a sense of peace and harmony between the co-mediators and that this is part of what generates an atmosphere which is conducive to resolving the conflict.

A further strength is obtained by two **complementary** mediators working together. This refers to the richness of the combined skills, experiences and personalities of the mediators. There are significant benefits to be had from mediators from different disciplines working together e.g. a combination of financial and legal expertise, commercial and medical etc.. Both mediators can bring their individual knowledge and experience to bear on the mediation process, resulting in a more comprehensive and creative process than in the case of a sole practitioner.

Working with an established partner deepens the level of harmony and the complementary aspect of the working relationship. It is important that the co mediators share a common vision of the process and that each recognises and appreciates their mutual strengths, skills and knowledge base. This is achieved through the experience of working together and learning from each other. It is achieved by understanding and respecting each other's values, needs and regard for the other's abilities and skills which are further developed and deepened through ongoing and shared reflective practice. To work with a co-mediator with whom you can develop this type of relationship is very rewarding and in our experience leads to a richer mediation experience.

Another central term to which we will refer in our discussion of co-mediation is '*dispute*'. We define it for the purposes of this discussion as:

> *'A stated conflict or controversy of claims or rights between two or more parties in relation to commercial, employment, community or family related matters'*

We will refer to the generic term 'dispute' as it relates to numerous subject areas including two party and multi-party commercial disputes, employment disputes, those in the community between neighbours or community organisations and private family related matters such as separating couples, inheritance issues or other family based disputes. Where we refer to the term generally it can be understood that the particular methods or discussion to which we refer has broad application across these areas.

The Amicus Model

Within any given mediation there are three key activities which need to be managed by the mediators. Zariski A. (2005) identifies three 'tracks of thought' running through a mediators mind during a mediation:

1. the **mediation process** – time keeping, sequence, physical environment

2. the interpersonal **dynamics between the parties** – analysing statements, absorbing emotions, determining conflict patterns

3. the **mediators' reflective practice** – maintaining awareness of their own reactions and responses to the mediation as the mediation unfolds

The figure below illustrates the Amicus Private Practice Co-mediation Model. It demonstrates the standard structure and processes which we follow while allowing for a level of flexibility required.

Amicus Private Practice Co-Mediation Model: Fig 1.

Reflective Practice

Managing
Interpersonal
Dynamics

Stages	Contact Mediator	Non-Contact Mediator
First Contact:	First contact Case Assessment ⇄	Case Assessment
Pre-Mediation:	Manages the process	
	Conducts meetings	Attends/conducts meetings if required
	Prepares for Mediation with non-contact mediator ⇄	Prepares for Mediation with contact mediator
Mediation:		
Welcome and Ground rules	Support →	Leads*
Opening Statements	Leads ←	Support
Story Telling	Support →	Leads
Exploring Options	Leads ←	Support
Agreement	Support ←	Leads
Post Mediation:	Manages outstanding matters	

Reflective
Practice

(* It is standard that the non-contact mediator will lead the opening stage of the mediation. The remaining sequence of lead and support mediator may be arranged differently than that set out above, depending upon the nature of the mediation)

Managing the Mediation Process

The mediation process begins at the enquiry stage and moves through a number of steps including first contact, pre-mediation, mediation and post mediation.

First contact – a mediation enquiry is normally made to either one of us. The 'contact mediator' to whom the initial contact is made will discuss the case with the party, explain the process and make arrangements for follow up. Having made an early assessment of the case and obtained agreement from each party to meet separately, the mediators will discuss the case and determine whether they deem it necessary for both to be present at the pre-mediation meetings. In the majority of cases, the pre-mediation meetings will be conducted by the 'contact mediator'. The exceptions to this include situations which are particularly complex and benefit from the skill set and support of the second mediator or where there is a multi-party dispute which require more management and resources.

Pre-mediation: We attach great significance to the pre-mediation stage. There are a number of steps that we follow:

1. Introductions and development of rapport
   Where the contact mediator conducts pre-mediation alone she will make reference to her co-mediator in a way that normalises the co-mediation concept from the outset. Where both mediators attend the pre-mediation, they each take the opportunity to communicate directly with the client to establish rapport and trust.

133

2. Obtaining an account of the party's perspective
   The purpose of this step is to elicit the background of the dispute and the perspective of the individual party. In more complex or multi-party mediations the combined skills of the two mediators will prove more efficient and fruitful as both mediators may conduct separate meetings at the same time.

3. Exploring options and developing mutuality
   Mutuality is a concept developed by the CINERGY® conflict coaching model and used by us in our coaching management work but also throughout the mediation process. Mutuality begins with the 'act of stepping into the other person's shoes' (Noble C. 2012) and thereby exploring the various elements of a conflict for both the client and the other person. The concept of gaining insights and understanding about these elements for both sides of the situation, 'is integral to helping clients understand the dynamic between themselves and the other person' (Noble C, 2007). Through our use of CINERGY® Conflict Management Coaching principles, we enable each party to begin to consider a new awareness/ perspective of the dispute and possible outcomes that may be achieved. Where we are both present at this stage we work from a shared methodology in a complementary way. This is the benefit of working with an established co-mediator partner with a common approach.

4. Obtaining agreement to mediate
   Agreement to mediate is obtained in writing by the signing of a formal document by the party and the mediators.

5. Next steps and preparation for mediation
   The 'contact mediator' will make the mediation arrangements with the parties including obtaining documents relevant to mediation, where necessary, and assistance with opening statements.

Where possible we will meet with the parties to the mediation at least once. Where it is not possible to meet due to geography or schedules, we will conduct our pre-mediation consultation by phone. In some cases it may be judged necessary to involve the second mediator at the pre-mediation stage. This can be particularly beneficial for multi-party mediations. The benefits of having a second mediator involved in pre-mediation when dealing with multi-party mediations is two-fold. Firstly, two heads can be better than one when there is a complex set of relationships and sizeable feedback and content to absorb. Secondly, significant time can also be saved in this type of dispute by the mediators sharing the task of meetings.

> Example –
>
> *We were asked to mediate in a dispute for a non-profit organisation. There were a number of parties involved including staff, directors and an external organisation. We needed to meet with 4 parties with a number of individuals in each one who were all involved in the disputes to varying degrees but who would also form an important part of the future agreement to be put in place for the development of the organisation. In this case we agreed between us the nature of what was to be discussed with each party and divided the pre-mediation meetings between us.*

It can also be beneficial to involve the second mediator in cases which are particularly complex and can benefit from the skill set of the non-contact mediator or where there are strong emotions involved which require greater management than normal. The interventions and observations of two mediators can result in a more comprehensive treatment and assessment of the case. It can also be an important part of building trust where a party is feeling particularly emotional and vulnerable about entering into mediation.

When the pre-mediation process is undertaken by one of us, we will then meet together with our partner to report on our findings. Together we will highlight the significant aspects of the case which we need to be mindful of in planning the mediation session. During pre-mediation the 'contact mediator' will maintain that role. She will communicate directly with the parties in relation to pre-mediation documents if required, the practical arrangements for the mediation session(s), and address and manage any other concerns or questions which the parties may have.

Mediation – The mediation session itself is co-mediated by us. The mediation session will be planned by us in advance and entails a number of steps/identifiable phases within the process. These include:

1. Welcome and setting the ground rules
2. Opening statements
3. Identify the Issues
4. Development of options
5. Agreement

Using the Amicus Private Practice Co-Mediation Model, the mediation will be opened and the welcome phase managed by the 'non-contact' mediator. This allows for the 'non-contact' mediator to establish a working rapport with the clients early on as the mediator may not have had an opportunity to meet the clients before hand (this will not be the case where it is decided to both attend the pre-mediation stage, but the rule will still apply). She will however be inclusive of the contact mediator, using 'we' instead of 'I' and inviting the contact mediator to add anything she may wish to or is relevant at this stage. This establishes the team approach from the beginning.

The contact mediator retains an overall managemment function throughout the entire mediation process e.g. her role is to ensure that all relevant documentation is obtained, that each step in the process if completed, that critical notes are maintained and the final agreement drafted (by the mediators themselves and/or other non-parties e.g. solicitors which may be present). The lead role will alternate between the mediators from step to step. It should be noted that where one of the mediators leads a particular phase of the mediation, it does not preclude the other from engaging with the clients during this phase, rather the lead mediator will merely lead the discussion and ensure that it has been completed. The lead mediator will also indicate to the other mediator when they feel it is appropriate to move on.

The task of note taking will be agreed between the co-mediators before the mediation begins. Most mediations will involve a level of work with the flip-chart which can also be used to record important aspects of the agreement. This work will also alternate between the mediators. In most instances note taking will be the particular responsibility of the contact mediator who will normally take primary responsibility for drafting the final agreement.

Whatever the arrangements you put in place in relation to the roles and responsibilities of each partner, it is important that they are pre planned and agreed between you.

> *'Where co-mediators operate in sync with one another, have the same vision of the mediation process and its goals, and have a plan that maximises the strengths of the mediation team, their combined talents increase their capacity to respond to the myriad challenges they will face'* (Love L. and Stulberg J., Pg 179)

Post-mediation: The post mediation communication with the parties is primarily the responsibility of the 'contact mediator', unless requested otherwise by the party(ies). In Family mediation this phase can be significant. The mediated agreement can be lengthy. In some instances there may be queries/follow up which is handled by the 'contact mediator'.

Managing the Interpersonal Dynamics between the Parties

Managing the interpersonal dynamics between the parties to a dispute can be challenging. It is critical to the success of the mediation that this is done effectively and in a way which encourages improved communication between, and affords every opportunity for the parties to discover new perspectives which align more favourably with a positive outcome for both parties. The ideal outcome would be one which provides a new and positive basis upon which agreement can be obtained and where parties experience a healing of the past conflict. In all cases this is not possible but as a minimum the mediators will strive to achieve a working agreement which enables both parties to move on.

In this context, the interpersonal dynamics between the parties to the dispute must be at the centre of the mediation and foremost throughout in the mind of the mediators. At every step in the mediation the mediators work with these dynamics, at times reframing the communication, introducing new ways of communicating, challenging each party through skilful questioning in a way that provokes each party to review and reconsider their perspective and explore new options for the future. In order to do this effectively the mediators need to:

- Listen actively and observe reactions
- Manage the expression of strong emotions
- Enable the parties to understand the perspective of the other
- Focus the clients on mutually beneficial options for the future

Working with an established partner in co-mediation can greatly enhance the mediators' ability to manage the interpersonal dynamics between the parties including those tasks specifically outlined above.

- Listen actively and observe reactions

If the mediator is to effectively manage the interpersonal dynamics between the parties in dispute, they must listen actively and observe each party and the pattern of interaction between them. This is particularly challenging in the early stages of mediation where each party is experiencing a heightened level of anxiety for the outcomes and the process. The mediator needs to be able to focus on the behaviour and needs of each party and establish a rapport and trust with each one that will support the resolution process.

Runde and Flanagan's views on this as it relates to leadership are as relevant for mediators,

> *'The key to applying this understanding of the dynamics of conflict lies in the ability to observe and detect a myriad of subtle human interaction cues. A raised eyebrow here or strain in the voice there may be the clues that alert the conflict competent leader to the potential conflict lurking just below the surface. The real trick is to monitor the clues and decide just how to respond' (Runde C. and Flanagan T., 2007)*

Co-mediation can be particularly helpful at this point in the mediation in that the lead mediator can listen actively and observe the parties and their responses to one another. The non-lead mediator can take notes and focus on the content of what is being said. They also act as a second 'pair of eyes' which provides a more comprehensive assessment particularly of the dynamics between the parties. Where a shuttle mediation is being conducted, it can be very useful for the mediators to have a brief discussion at this point, to share their observations and quickly determine the critical aspects of the interpersonal dynamics at play.

In the case of a joint mediation i.e. where the parties are together in the same room with the mediators, it can be very helpful for the non-lead mediator to repeat and reframe where necessary, the key points of the opening statements. This gives the lead mediator an opportunity to reflect on their observations and assess how to proceed to the next phase i.e. Identify the Issues.

- Manage the expression of strong emotions

This is another important task which the mediators must do. When handled well it can greatly increase the sense of trust felt by the party towards the mediator(s). Through establishing their presence with the person the mediator can determine how long to let the person vent, when to acknowledge their emotions, how to help them to communicate in a different way with the other party and to assess at what point to begin to challenge the party to look at the conflict from a wider perspective.

> *'Sometimes it may be necessary to let a conflict escalate somewhat, enough to deal with emotions but not so much as to impair people's ability to eventually deal with the situation constructively. The art of dealing with conflict often lies in finding the narrow path between useful expression of emotions and destructive polarization' (Mayer B., 2000:11).*

In co-mediation this can be done very successfully. The non-lead mediator can also observe the behaviour of both parties during this time. A second mediator can sometimes pick up on subtleties and body language that a lead mediator may miss and can therefore make useful interventions.

Another advantage of co-mediation is that it is less inclined to generate partiality in the mediator. During mediations the parties can often try to win favour with the mediator and expend significant energy in 'winning over' the mediator to their position, particularly where there are strong emotions involved. With a second mediator present this intensive interaction can be diluted as the interventions are shared by the mediators. This keeps the interaction more open and focused on the issues rather than the personalities, enabling the mediators to remain more neutral and less judgemental.

In order for the mediators to work effectively in the management of strong emotions it is essential that they share a common methodology and skill. This is developed over time with an established co-mediator partner. They must both be aware of the sequence and flow of the mediation and each stage of the process. In this way they must work together complementing each other's interventions and efforts.

- Enable the parties to understand the perspective of the other

Disputes arise between parties who hold incompatible perspectives in relation to a given situation. It is critical therefore that mediation can work at the level of changing perspectives so as to ensure that the parties move towards a more compatible perspective. Working at the level of perspective change is challenging and needs significant focus and concentration on the part of the mediator.

In co mediation this work can be shared thereby relieving the mediators when they need a break and reinforcing each other to greater effect. The mediators will work in sync with a party who is giving their perspective, each asking questions and giving input as they see fit. This can be helpful in keeping the party talking openly as their focus turns to two different sets of questions and a broader range of discussion. Each mediator will have a different approach and understanding of the issues based on their own background and personality and so it can provide a more comprehensive treatment of the situation.

This can be useful where there is a complex set of circumstances and where each mediator can bring different knowledge and skills to the situation e.g. where there is a complex set of financial details within a contractual relationship – it is good to have the input of mediators with both financial and legal expertise.

From time to time we will discuss with each other aspects of the process. This can set the working tone of the mediation which we hope the parties will emulate. This can be very useful where parties are finding it difficult to communicate with each other or where one or more of the parties are aggressive in their approach

- Focus parties on mutually beneficial options for the future

Creativity is key to reaching agreement and/or resolution in a mediation. With established co-mediation partners the mediators will be highly tuned to each other and inspire a sense of an open and creative working environment in which all parties can contribute equally and be heard. It is here that co mediation in our experience excels. As the mediation process moves into the consideration of future options, both parties must be encouraged to consider all possibilities and the pros and cons of each. In most cases at this stage we would use a flip chart to capture the various ideas and proposals made.

One mediator will take on the role of writing on the flip chart and both will ask questions and provide input as they determine appropriate and useful. We will exchange roles again according to the needs of the mediation. In Family mediation we may change as we move from the Financial Plan to the Parental Plan, in other mediations we may change as we move from one issue to the next. In all cases we will have a pre agreed format for doing this. That is not to say that during a given mediation we may not prompt each other to take over if we are losing energy or need a break.

Having two mediators present at this stage means that there are two minds exploring issues which is more beneficial than one. They bring different experiences, knowledge and perspectives to bear on the problem. They also generate a creative dynamic by asking different types of questions, being more attentive to the parties views and stimulating greater levels of discussion of issues than would be the case with a sole mediator.

> *'When co mediators work on a case together, the give-and-take of direct personal communication is increased and often is critical in the closing of a settlement'* *(Epstein J. and Epstein S., 2006, Vol 35, No 6/22)*

Reflective Practice

Reflective practice hones and develops our skills as mediators. It is something which we all need to do both within the mediation process and afterwards. Our awareness of our own reactions and responses can determine the extent of our success in mediation. We are all human and when we work with people in conflict, it can be very challenging at a personal level. In our opinion we must be authentic and present to our clients in mediation in a neutral and positive way. Without these key elements we are not as open to resolution and can become part of the conflict dynamic between the parties.

Throughout the mediation process we will aim to maintain rapport and trust with the parties, retain our neutrality, maintain high levels of concentration and energy, be positive and maintain a belief that agreement is possible. These are the personal attributes we bring to mediation. Co mediation supports reflective practice in that it:

- provides you with an opportunity to discuss your own responses with your co-mediator

- provides a form of peer supervision

- can compensate for any lapses or shortcomings in our own responses

143

Sometimes in a mediation, there may can be scenarios or issues discussed that provoke a reaction in the mediator. This can colour your view of the individual party or introduce a level of bias consciously or otherwise. Once this happens you become a less effective mediator. In co mediation it can be very helpful to discuss what is happening with your co mediator. This can be done between caucuses in a shuttle mediation or at a recess when mediating jointly. Sometimes when the issue is voiced and discussed it can be resolved, other times it may not be but your co mediator once aware of the situation can compensate and redress the impact if any on the mediation.

Co-mediation operates as a form of ongoing peer supervision. Through working together over time we are both very conscious and aware of the other's values, skills and reactions. We trust each other during times when we need to discuss aspects of our approach or responses within mediation. By the mere presence of another mediator we are also prompted to be more conscious of the personal attributes we bring to the mediation and remain more accountable to demonstrating and achieving excellence in what we do and how we perform our role.

When you co-mediate with an established partner, you will become tuned to their personality and you will quickly pick up on their reactions to situations. You will sense their comfort or otherwise and their energy levels as you mediate. Both partners are well placed to read the situation and to intervene when they feel it is necessary to compensate or support the other who may need it.

Example –

Phil and I were mediating with a separating couple. They had both undergone a lengthy period of separation. Each time they approached what appeared to be an agreement between themselves in the past, things had broken down. Phil and I had worked hard with both parties in pre-mediation and within the mediation itself. After a long day's work in which most aspects of the agreement appeared to be in place, there was one item which related to their future accommodation which could not be finalised on the day. We had put in place a plan A,B and C depending upon what emerged in the following weeks, regarding their property sales/purchases, which would address this issue. As though from nowhere, one of the parties began to get very critical of the mediation process which could not finalise this matter. I immediately felt a wave of reaction in myself to what I considered to be a most unfair comment. My own sensitivity to what I interpreted as an unjust criticism was creating a negative reaction in me. With one glance at Phil she immediately intervened in a very calm and positive way. She deflected a reaction in me which could have undermined the agreement which was almost complete. Instead I could gather my energy and regain my positivity. Although one party didn't make as much progress as she wished, we did end the mediation with a working agreement and a positive outlook for the future.

The Advantages of Co-Mediation

In conclusion, the benefits of working with an established co-mediation partner are numerous. It provides

-   a second pair of eyes, ears and hands, which working in unison can manage and inform the mediation process with greater efficiency than a sole practitioner

- it brings two sets of skills, knowledge and experience to the table generating more creative solutions

- it generates a harmonious working atmosphere which is conducive to conflict resolution

- it creates a higher level of positive energy maintained by two mediators who support each other through sharing tasks

- it provides a level of peer supervision between the mediators maintaining greater neutrality and authenticity in both mediators which will have a significant impact on the conflict resolution process

By working together over time we have found that we continually learn from one another. We constantly discover and rediscover each other's skills and abilities and are inspired by the insights and energy that we both bring to mediation. It enables us to maintain a positive and impartial perspective in our work and in our experience creates greater opportunity for agreement and/or resolution of the disputes we mediate.

We would encourage all mediators to explore the benefits of co-mediation. Our practice is built on the co-mediation model. There is a distinct sense of absence when we mediate alone, which is now seldom. Co-mediation with an established partner has a flow and dynamic to it which can be magical and inspire and support positive outcomes for those in dispute.

References:

Newmark C. and Monaghan A., Butterworths (2005) *'Mediators on Mediation: Leading Mediator Perspectives on the Practice of Commercial Mediation'*, Tottel

Bowling D. and Hoffman D., (2003)'*Bringing Peace Into the Room*', Jossey-Bass

Zariski A. , Text of a presentation to the Western Australian Dispute Resolution Association Seminar, October 25, 2005

Noble C. (2012), '*Conflict Management Coaching: The CINERGY ™ Model*', CINERGY™ Coaching

Noble C., CINERGY® Conflict Management Coaching Workshop, 2007

Runde C. and Flanagan T., (2007) '*Becoming a Conflict Competent Leader*', Jossey-Bass

Mayer B., (2000), '*The Dynamics of Conflict Resolution: A Practitioner's Guide*', Jossey Bass

Epstein J. and Epstein S. , '*The Colorado Lawyer*', June 2006, Vol 35, No6/22

Love L. and Stulberg J., '*Practice Guidelines for Co-Mediation: Making Certain That 'Two Heads Are Better Than One*', Vol 13, Issue 3, 1996

10. Co-Mediation as part of a Mediation and Conflict Coaching Pairing

Monica Hanaway

Introduction

In this chapter I shall explore a case example, in which through unforeseen circumstances, one member of the co-mediation duo was unable to be present on the middle day of a three day mediation.

This chapter also covers the use of conflict coaching on a one to one basis as an integral part of a mediation process – how this was addressed in the case described and how coaching can take place as part of the pre or post mediation work and the potential benefits and drawbacks within a co-mediation model.

The case

The company in which I am a co-director encourages organizations to think proactively and use conflict coaching when change is planned, as change almost always provokes conflict. However, we tend to be called in when there is a crisis and mediation is required. Most of my mediations are carried out with my co-mediator with whom I work regularly and with whom I share a high degree of understanding. We share the role of lead mediator equally between us. However, unforeseen circumstances can throw us challenges which mean we have to adapt our model.

One example of this was when we were called into a large organisation to mediate between two work colleagues, Jane and Sarah, who were very stuck in a dispute, following a large restructuring programme within the company. Various interventions from more senior colleagues in the organisation and from the HR department had failed to elicit any movement on either side. Initially we agree to try a one day mediation, there was no opportunity to extend the agreed time as prior commitments meant both my colleague and I had to fly back immediately after the close of the mediation. During the mediation the real sources of the dispute began to be clarified and we were able to agree a resolution to some aspects of the conflict and signpost a way forward.

The first phase: The Mediation

Pre-work

In the first phase of the mediation my co-mediator and I followed our usually model of working together with the parties in dispute. I took the lead in the pre-mediation process, speaking to both parties by phone in the weeks leading up to the mediation. Jane was very sceptical about the usefulness of mediation and felt that her management role was being challenged by the organisation's decision to bring in external mediators to deal with an issue she felt she should be able to resolve. She did not express much willingness to engage in the process but felt she had no option but to attend. Sarah was more emotional during these calls and keen for the opportunity she saw the mediation as presenting.

Background to the dispute

The background to the dispute focused on the fallout from the recent restructuring. The two parties were required to work closely together. Jane had recently taken up the post as Sarah's line manager, following a major restructuring in which both had faced possible redundancy or redeployment.

Before the restructure, they had been on the same level in the organization. Sarah had worked independently managing an IT section. Reluctantly she had accepted a move to an administrative post. Jane had moved from a PA role to manage five staff, of whom Sarah was one.

Day 1: mediation

As I had undertaken the pre-work my co-mediator took the lead at the start of the mediation. He made the introductions, emphasised the mediator's role as being non-judgemental, open and neutral, set the ground rules re confidentiality and respect, checked any limits to the authority to settle held by those attending and took Jane and Sarah through the practicalities of how the day would run, with the use of both private caucus sessions and joint sessions when appropriate. This leading role allowed the focus to shift from me, as the person they had already spoken with, to my co-mediator thus pulling him into the process and allowing the parties' time to settle with his presence.

This mediation focused on the breakdown in the working relationship between Jane and Sarah. Jane considered Sarah, to be a 'slacker', doing the minimum amount of work possible, being reluctant to tell Jane what she was doing because 'she probably wasn't doing anything' and questioning Jane's authority. In turn, Sarah considered Jane a 'jobsworth' with no management experience. Jane's post had never been advertised and Jane had, in Sarah's words, 'merely been given the post'. In the mediation, Jane confirmed this, saying 'a new post had been created for me.'

Jane had little training to prepare her for the new management role and it became clear that she saw this as a unique opportunity to move into management. She was determined that she be accepted as a manager and awarded the respect she felt was due to the managerial status.

Sarah found Jane's managerial style overbearing. She was irritated that whenever she asked Jane why she was being asked to do something, Jane replied, 'Because I tell you to, and I am your boss'. Sarah felt she had experience which could be useful to Jane but that Jane refused to consult anyone or respect team members.

Throughout the mediation my co-mediator and I stayed together and took turns in leading the process. We were both able to establish a good working relationship with both sides. In a break a spoke to my co-mediator about the ways in which Jane reminded me of an old manager of mine who I had felt was not cut out for management and I asked my colleague to alert me if I showed any favouritism to Sarah's situation. The co-mediation model allows for each co-mediator to act as an informal supervisor to their partner. Obviously for this to work both of the mediators has to trust, respect and feel save with their partner.

At the end of a fairly tough day's mediation Jane and Sarah reached agreement on a number of issues. However, many issues had been raised which could not be fully explored within the time constraint. Some of these issues were personal and the parties were reluctant to discuss them with their employers, others flowed from the lack of experience and training which should have followed on to fit both parties for their new roles. For these reasons, it was agreed that coaching would take place with both parties separately and then a further day would be set aside to bring them together for a second mediation session to agree an acceptable behaviour contract (ABC).

This presented us with a further and new challenge. The organisation was keen that the coaching should happen soon over the course of one day and the second mediation aimed at drawing up the ABC should follow on the next day. Unfortunately my co-mediator was unable to attend the coaching day due to an important prior commitment. This was the first occasion when we had started work as co-mediators where circumstances required that one of us must work alone for the second day of a three-day process.

We discussed the possible problems this may present. We were concerned that my co-mediator may feel, or in fact be, side-lined in some way when he returned for the third day. It was possible that the coaching may result in a very firm bond being established between me and one or both parties. Another concern was that I would have acquired information which was new to him, thus handicapping him or placing him in a secondary role. I was also aware that I would be without his monitoring of any possible projection of feelings I might have onto either party.

It was essential we discussed these concerns openly and we were able to plan accordingly. We could have chosen for me to carry out the coaching on my own and also to act as sole mediator for the third day. However, we agreed that my co-mediator would fly back immediately after fulfilling his commitment which meant that he would arrive late on the evening of the day's coaching. This would allow me time to fully brief him on what had been achieved in his absence and of any concerns which had arisen. His presence on the third day also allowed for us to have a strategy to cover any issues or breakdowns which may have occurred between me and either party during the coaching phase.

Day 2: The coaching phase

Jane had been insistent that the main issue was Sarah's 'insubordination', 'secrecy' and 'lack of engagement with the work' and that Sarah needed 'to do as she was told and not question it'. Through the coaching, I was able to introduce Jane to a model of explorative listening. She experienced the power of being listened to and the power of feeling the authentic desire of the listener to understand. She was then able to employ these skills in her subsequent meetings with Sarah.

In the coaching we were able to explore what lay at the heart of the frustration both parties felt with the other and how this seemed to stem from a clash in value systems. Through our work during the day we were able to identify some areas of commonality in their value systems which my co-mediator and I had noted at the end of the first day. Both shared a strong belief that one should be rewarded for good behaviour. However they differed in what they believed to be 'good behaviour'.

During the coaching sessions I was able to learn more about Jane. She had a high achieving husband, who was often away on business, so she would return to an empty house after work. She was encouraging of her husband's ambition but wanted to match his success. She spoke movingly of dinner parties where she had felt she had little to offer to the high powered conversation, lowering her self-esteem and hoped that this would change now that she too was 'a manager with staff working to him'.

Jane's self-esteem was heavily invested in the new managerial role. She resented the fact that Sarah did not seem to recognise her status and saw work as less important to home life.

It unfolded in the individual sessions with Sarah that she had a partner with a serious long term illness and so stuck very closely to her contracted working hours so that she could spend as much time as possible with him. One of Sarah's complaints was that Jane never enquired about his partner's health even though she was aware of the situation.

Through our dialogue Jane realized that she too might wish to go home on time if there was someone waiting for her. In many ways she too resented how much time and energy work was taking and acknowledged that part of her would like to be more self-disciplined (a word she never thought he would use about Sarah) and set aside at least one evening a week for some non-work relate activity, just as Sarah attended her evening course.

She spoke with concern about the Sarah's husband's health but expressed her view that Sarah was a very private person who would not wish her difficulties to be spoken about at work. In thinking further about this she began to understand that her perceived lack of interest in Sarah's home situation was experienced as cold, uncaring and disrespectful and so was having an impact on their working relationship. She resolved to 'be brave' and to occasionally 'check in' with Sarah about how her husband was doing. In understanding that Sarah's priorities lay in the home, Jane also saw that Sarah was not a competitor to her on the career ladder.

This allowed Jane to be brave enough to share with me her fears for the future. A further restructure was due, with her employers taking over another organisation. Jane knew that the person occupying her role in the other organisation was an experienced and well trained manager who was held in high regard and she feared that the merger would result in her redundancy or demotion. Jane's complaints about her management style had been threatening on many levels but she feared that she would be seen as an ineffective manager and so had become increasingly more demanding and authoritarian in the hope that she could 'force Jane into line'. Although it was clear that this was having the opposite effect to the one hoped for, with Sarah digging her heels in deeper, Jane had no experience, management training or knowledge to draw on and felt stuck, disheartened and scared.

Sarah too expressed common feelings of fear, frustration and stuckness. She had no knowledge of Jane's insecurity and saw her merely as a bully. She could not understand why Jane responded so defensively to any questions she posed as to why they were doing things in a certain way. In he coaching piece with Jane, she began to see that Sarah's questions were no threat and that she could choose how to respond to them. She began to see strength in admitting that there were things she did not know and understand that my owning this she could effectively use the skills and knowledge of others whilst building on her own knowledge.

Most of my work with Sarah focused on exploring her communication style and helping her so see that she too could be experienced as aggressive. She was also able to forceful express her anger at the way she felt she had been treated by the organisation and realise that much of this anger was being projected onto Jane.

Both recognised that they had been thrown into new roles without any training and both felt unsure about their abilities in these roles. They began to recognise that they were both 'victims' of the restructure and that they had much in common.

With Jane, I was able to offer some brief leadership coaching, sharing key approaches which she could call on to help her achieve her objectives. She identified that through the lack of knowledge of other approaches and her own feelings of inadequacy she had automatically taken on a very transactional, directive style which emphasised punishment for non-compliance. To adopt a more questioning transformational approach, allowing others to question her actions would have made her feel very vulnerable, to exposing her lack of experience and knowledge. I introduced her to Connective and Existential Leadership theories and the concept of Negative Capability within which leaders no longer have to hold onto the illusion that they can solve all problems.

The coaching day turned out to be rich in learning for both parties and myself. This meant there was a lot for me to feedback to my co-mediator from what had been an exhausting day.

Day 3

We discussed what the coaching had focused on and the possible levels of understanding and behavioural changes which had occurred. We were very aware of how Jane had changed during this phase. She had moved from a very cynical distanced stance which she had stayed with during the first day's mediation, to allowing me to see her vulnerabilities and fears and showing a willingness to train and understand management and leadership strategies. However, we needed to respect that Jane had not shown this side of herself to my co-mediator.

In normal circumstances I would have handed the lead role back to my co-mediator to ensure his full involvement and reconnection with the parties, following his absence. However, we agreed that although he would start by reintroducing himself and acknowledging that a lot of work had happened whilst he wasn't there, he would then take a very reactive stance and wait to see how the parties chose to include or exclude him. This is a very strong position for the co-mediator to take. It would be easy to feel the need to boost our own self esteem by making our presence felt, to make up for the fact that people seemed to have managed fine without us. My co-mediator is very experienced and self-aware and so did not feel threatened by the secondary role he felt he should occupy at the beginning of day three. He very sensitively took a back seat.

As the day progressed, the parties seemed to forget that he had not been present on the second day. They openly talked to each other about their shared frustrations with the organisation. They were able to identify and tell one another what they admired in the other. Jane was able to talk sensitively to Sarah about her husband's illness and for Sarah to receive this as genuine concern rather than pointing out a weakness. My co-mediator very perceptively entered more into the dialogue as the day proceeded. He was careful not to allude to any knowledge which he had acquired through our briefing session, (although the party had been made fully aware that it had happened), sticking to what was being openly shared during the day.

The mediation concluded with an agreed plan for the ways in which the parties would resume working together. They had learnt more about who they each were as individuals and what was important for each of them in life. Working models for achieving the best outcome for work goals were identified and as both had ceased to see the other as a threat they were able to establish a positive way of communicating.

Conclusion

This case brought into focus some key elements in co-mediating practice. The first and most important for me was the choice of co-mediator. My co-mediator and I work together on a very regular basis. We are co-founders and co-directors of our mediation company. On a very concrete note we are keen to provide excellence in mediation practice for our own self-esteem and for the reputation of our company – it is far more than just 'a job' for both of us.

We are both equally strongly committed to mediation as the most effective, positive and developmental way to resolve conflict. In our professional lives we have experienced poor management of conflict and seen the escalating negative results for the companies and individuals involved. Then again, we have worked with companies who work proactively, anticipating structural changes which may lead to uncertainty and conflict in their workforce and planning how to lessen anxiety and reduce conflict. On one occasion we were lucky enough to work with a large global company who had a clear five year strategy which would eventually require redundancies. They invested in work with their senior executives to ensure that they were aware of conflict management and conflict resolution approaches and skills in addition to running a well thought through communication strategy to ensure everyone was aware of planned changes and why these needed to happen.

In the case of Jane and Sarah, I believe the process benefited from the fact that both my co-mediator and I are qualified and experienced existential psychotherapists as well as coaches and mediators. For Jane and Sarah much of the dispute was not about the concrete day to day relationships within the workplace but about issues of self-identity, tensions re priorities and fears for the future.

As mediators we both understand the importance of these psychological issues which often block rational solutions being easily found. Our shared training and philosophical stance means that we can tolerate our co-mediator exploring an area which at first seems far removed from the dispute allowing them the free rein to run with any theme which is introduced by the client.

To take the backseat when our co-mediator has establish rapport with the client means having the ability to repress the inner voice which may be shouting 'you don't look very important here' or 'if this works it will seem as though it is entirely due to your co-mediator'. Our self-esteem and job satisfaction may feel threatened. Being able to be silent and refraining from intervening can be very difficult but is an important skill in mediation. Equally the skill of knowing when to enter into the dialogue is essential; to know when to move to the foreground to give your co-mediator a break or allow for a different perspective to be introduced. The mediation between Jane and Sarah really challenged this aspect of our working partnership. The central day in the absence of my co-mediator had placed me squarely in the lead role. My co-mediator was accepting of this and worked accordingly with the dynamics this set up. He very sensitively played an essential part in the third day of the mediation never striving to impose his presence. This gentle approach allowed both parties to continue to feel safe about the vulnerabilities they had shared with me and went on to share many of them with each other and my co-mediator over the course of that third day.

The process highlighted the issue of confidentiality. Although both parties knew that my co-mediator would be absent for one day and that I would brief him before the final day, we were very aware that quite personal matters had been shared in day 2. We were clear that neither I nor my co-mediator would allude to these issues until they were brought into the mediation. The client was empowered to share as much or as little of what had been discussed. My co-mediator's sensitive way of re-entering the mediation process meant that both parties were not over aware of his presence and gradually shared almost all of what had been discussed the previous day.

If I had been working with a mediator I knew less well would the mediation have worked? I shall never know the answer to this, but I do know that my trust in my co-mediator and our very proactive and explicit discussion of potential challenges meant that the mediation provided us with an excellent learning opportunity and an excellent outcome for our clients.

References

Bass, B. M. (1985), *'Leadership and performance beyond expectation'*. New York: Free Press.

Bass B. M. (1990) From Transactional to Transformational Leadership: Learning to Share the Vision. *Organizational Dynamics* Winter: p.19-31

Burns, J. M. (1978), *'Leadership'*. New York: Harper & Row

French R. (2000) *Negative Capability, Dispersal and the Containment of Emotion* Robert French: Bristol Business School, University of the West of England http://www.ispso.org/Symposia/London/2000French.htm

Koestenbaum P. & Block B., (2001), *'Freedom and Accountability at Work: Applying Philosophic Insight to the Real World'* Jossey Bass

Lipman-Blumen J. (1996) *Connective Leadership* Oxford: Oxford University Press

11. Co-mediation in cross-cultural settings

Judith McKimm-Vorderwinkler

Introduction

This chapter looks at co-mediation in cross-cultural settings, where truly understanding people's worldviews can be a difficult, yet crucial issue. By their very nature, understanding one another depends not only on language but also on a series of defining cultural variables. If these variables are not understood and dealt with in an adequate manner by the co-mediators, no effective communication can take place, making it be more difficult to build trust. The already existing anxiety in conflict may be aggravated, and the prospects of reaching an agreement will be diminished. A setting of this kind is a typical example of a situation in which co-mediating with a colleague who is an intercultural and language specialist becomes necessary.

The way emotions are perceived and expressed is culture-specific, and cultural variables determine people's behaviour as well as aspects of verbal and nonverbal expression. Conflict styles and communication strategies during conflict management processes are determined by one's culture, and culture as well as identity are strongly embedded in language – and vice-versa. Resorting to a common language by non-native speakers in cross-cultural communication may falsify their message, since the common language may lack the association with their own culture. Furthermore, speaking a foreign language in an emotionally charged situation can have psycholinguistic implications which need to be understood and managed appropriately. Being able to deal with these multiple factors in a mediation will ensure effective communication, allowing to build a relationship of trust, and giving the individuals in dispute the assurance of being truly heard.

Cultural homogeneity is becoming less and less the norm in today's globalised world. Almost every society has become multicultural to a greater or lesser degree. We have also become more interconnected since cross-border interpersonal relations take place at every level. More people travel, more people work in foreign countries, more people build personal relationships with members of other cultures than their own. As a result of this incremented mutual exposure, the probability of conflict arising between members from different cultural backgrounds is on the rise. For the purpose of this chapter, I refer to such conflicts as cross-cultural disputes, whether they occur in personal, professional or other relationships.

Since parties involved in cross-cultural disputes have different worldviews, and culture-specific variables determine their behaviour and perception, such conflicts can be characterised by complex dynamics. This is manifested in both verbal and non-verbal expressions which need to be properly decoded during a mediation in order to guarantee effective communication. Non-familiar, and therefore unintelligible means of expression may lead to misunderstandings, incorrect interpretations and inappropriate reactions on the part of the participants, obstructing the communication process and the building of trust.

Normally, 75% of oral communication is either misheard, misinterpreted or misunderstood (Apaydin, 2011). Since language and culture are intrinsically linked, it becomes evident that this percentage may increase when people from different linguistic and cultural backgrounds try to communicate. It is often assumed that speaking a common language may allow for verbal clarification of culturally conditioned differences. But each language is the means of expression of a particular worldview that may not be fully expressed in all its nuances through another language. The risk is always loss of content and consequently a lack of effective communication. This is particularly the case in situations where emotions come into play, since genuine emotional expression can only take place in a person's native language. Furthermore, the manifest nonverbal cultural expressions, which also define emotional expression, need to be understood and decoded correctly.

Such decoding of cultural expressions is a crucial issue in mediation settings since establishing and maintaining the needed trust with the parties depends on it. A mediator who, as hard as he/she may try, does not fully understand a person's culturally conditioned worldview, is not going to be able to mediate effectively. And I would suggest that a mediator who does not fully undestand a person's native "language world" cannot mediate effectively either. Therefore, a cross-cultural mediation requires specialised intercultural knowledge, in addition to a high degree of intercultural sensitivity and awareness, as well as linguistic capabilities and psychoinguistic understanding on the part of the mediator.

In order to assure balance and impartiality during the mediation of a cross-cultural dispute it is advisable to resort to co-mediation, whereby the mediators should either be members of the cultures in question, or have the above mentioned necessary intercultural and linguistic expertise. Having representatives of the respective groups or a cultural expert as mediator increases the prospect that all parties involved in the dispute are truly heard. Especially in cases where a party in dispute is a minority member in a dominant cultural environment, having a co-mediator with the necessary competencies to understand the foreigner's worldview can be a reassuring aspect which reduces the prospect of the foreign client from feeling marginalised, while helping him/her to feel being heard.

Cultural variables and emotions in conflict

The main defining factor for behaviour in conflict is whether individuals belong to what Hofstede (2005) has termed collectivistic or individualistic cultures. For collectivistic cultures, in all aspects in life, the individual is embedded in a group which looks after him/her in exchange for unconditioned loyalty. The group's overall wellbeing is more important than that of its single members. People tend to behave in such a way as to ensure group harmony and not to disrupt it by standing out. This is especially the case in Asian cultures, but it is also a typical characteristic of predominantly rural cultures too. Members of individualistic societies, on the other hand, tend to emphasize the individual, his/her capabilities, aspirations and interests. Ties between people are loose, looking after oneself and one's closest family members is the norm, and standing out through achievement and unique characteristics is encouraged and rewarded. According to Hofstede (2005), the majority of the world's societies are collectivistic. However, there are higher and lesser degrees of collectivism and individualism. Many Asian and some South American societies are among the most collectivistically oriented ones whereas the US are considered the most individualistic.

Emotions play a crucial part in conflict and it is through emotions that people's values and value systems find expression. Le Baron (2002) points out that people express and evaluate emotions according to significant cultural variations, insofar as some cultures condone strong emotional expression whereas others suppress or condemn it. Hall (1981) and Birdwhistell (1970) maintain that *'culture provides the basic rules that govern the when and how of what emotions should be expressed or concealed'* (cited in Ting-Toomey, 1999: 119).

Ting-Toomey (1999) studied the manifestation of emotions across cultures and her findings show that collectivistic cultures tend not to show their emotions overtly, especially with members of their own group. Even positive emotions tend to be displayed in a modest manner, and extreme negative emotions are suppressed altogether in order not to upset the group harmony. Because strong negative emotions tend to be suppressed, collectivists also are less able to decode negative facial expressions. In contrast, individualistic cultures tend to encourage the display of a wide range of both positive and negative emotions and their members are able to decode them accurately. These differences lead to the possibility that verbal and nonverbal cues of emotional expression, or the lack of such, are misinterpreted in intercultural encounters. An Asian person's restraint in showing emotions may seem alienating and untrustworthy to a stranger and convey the idea of coldness or lack of empathy. In reality, it is only the manner of expression which conceals the emotions. Asian collectivists, on the other hand, may regard the typically Western overt expression of emotions as a lack of maturity, restraint, and respect for others. Hasada (1997) notes that for the Japanese, controlling emotions is an important part of growth and showing emotions a sign of weakness. Strong emotional expressions such as crying are disdained since they cause embarrassment and insecurity to onlookers.

Nonverbal behaviour across cultures

Experts such as Birdwhistell (1955) and Mehrabian (1981) sustain that as much as two thirds of interactional meaning is transmitted through nonverbal messages. According to Ting-Toomey (1999), *'Nonverbal messages can oftentimes express what verbal messages cannot express and are assumed to be more truthful than verbal messages'* (Ting-Toomey, 1999: 115). It is, however, our culturally embedded experience that tells us how to interpret facial and eye expressions, gestures, personal space, and touch, and we rely on them in order to complete our interpretation of the conveyed message. Ting-Toomey (1999) gives examples of bodily gestures, such as hand gestures, which can carry different meanings, therefore causing misunderstandings and conflict. The 'OK' gesture in America (circle between thumb and forefinger), for instance, means 'money' in Japan, a sexual insult in Brazil and Greece, or 'zero' in France.

However, Ting-Toomey (1999) sustains that mostly, nonverbal behaviour relates to people's emotions. Ekman and Oster (1979) note that, while all human beings express emotions through nonverbal cues, it is culture to determine when, how, where, and with whom they should be expressed or suppressed. Therefore, nonverbal emotional behaviour can be misleading in cross-cultural situations. Using one's own nonverbal cultural frame in order to decode the others' message easily leads to misinterpretations and the message can even go unnoticed. These misinterpretations are also more difficult to rectify. Hasada (1997), for example, points out that lowering the gaze in Japanese culture means being pleased and satisfied about something whereas in Western societies it usually conveys sadness. Widening the eyes implies rudeness for the Japanese, whereas in Western societies it may signal astonishment or surprise. Furthermore, Ting-Toomey (1999) points out that avoiding eye-contact is a sign of showing respect for the Japanese and Native-Americans who interpret eye-contact as intrusive. By contrast, in the Western world, avoidance of eye-contact is seen as a sign of shyness or deviousness.

Smiling and laughter could be thought of as conveying universally valid messages. However, their meaning and circumstances are culture-specific; therefore awareness of subtle situational distinctions is required when dealing with members of certain cultures. In Japan, according to Hasada (1997), laughter can facilitate interaction but also fill uncomfortable pauses. Laughter can be used to punish and insult and can therefore hurt other people's feelings, so laughing freely is only allowed to children. Therefore, smiling is considered more appropriate. For the Japanese, a smile can, apart from establishing a warm and pleasant climate or signifying joy, mask embarrassment and displeasure, or suppress anger.

Conflict Styles

The cultural dimension of individualism-collectivism also influences their members' selection of certain conflict styles and determines the way in which conflict is managed. Stella Ting-Toomey's (1999) research shows that individualists adopt an outcome-oriented approach in dealing with conflict. In order to resolve a conflict effectively, personal opinions need to be expressed and acknowledged, and interests must be defined and clarified. Each side's goals must either be reached or compromised, and action plans must be drawn up for avoiding future trouble. In managing conflict, individualists tend to use more self-defensive, controlling and competitive styles. Neuliep (2006) points out that the emphasis is given to saving one's own face, either by giving it full priority or by integrating the other person's needs to save face while still stressing one's own. Collectivistic cultures, on the other hand, tend to adopt a process-oriented, indirect approach to conflict. They look at the 'big picture', decide how to resolve the problem, and analyse holistic contexts that have caused it. An important aspect for collectivists evolves around saving face through verbal and nonverbal messages. For collectivists, it is as important to uphold the other's honor, dignity, and prestige just as much as one's own. Conflict is effectively resolved when the parties contribute to saving face mutually while reaching a consensus between them. In order for conflict management to be seen as successful, collectivists expect subtle negotiations and strategic dealing in saving or upgrading face which is seen as more important as winning or losing a conflict.

Ting-Toomey's (1999) findings have shown that these different conflict styles create tensions and misinterpretation in cross-cultural encounters. Individualists tend to view collectivists' indirect conflict style as trying to avoid genuine discussion issues. Collectivists perceive individualists as too pushy, rude, overbearing and direct.

High- and Low-Context Communication

The manner in which people communicate also varies stylistically from culture to culture. In some cultures, people express a message in a more explicit and direct verbal way, whereas in others, most part of the message is conveyed through the nonverbal context. Hall (1976) describes these communication styles as *low-context* and *high-context*. Typical low-context cultures are usually individualistic ones, such as the US, Israel, or Germany. The message is conveyed in a direct and unambiguous manner. Most collectivistic cultures such as in Asia and some Latin-American countries, are considered high-context. The message is mostly conveyed indirectly and tends to lie 'between the lines'. It is often accompanied by nonverbal cues which need to be understood in order not to be missed.

Chua and Gudykunst (1987) argue that conflict resolution styles differ between low- and high-context cultures. Low-context cultures tend to separate the conflict issue from the persons involved, whereas for members of high-context cultures the conflict issue and the persons involved are strongly connected. This may manifest itself by the fact that disagreeing with someone is avoided because it may be seen as insulting and make both sides lose face. It may cause consternation and insecurity in a low-context speaker when a high-context individual seems reluctant to disagree directly and does not appear to show his/her true feelings overtly. This may be misinterpreted and come across as false and untrustworthy. In reality, the high-context speaker's intention is to save both his own and the other person's face. At the same time, individuals from high-context cultures may perceive the direct communication style of a low-context speaker as too insensitive and rude. Without intercultural knowledge and awareness, decoding the real content and intention behind the indirect, nonverbal, or the direct, verbal message may prove to be difficult and lead to the wrong conclusions.

Although knowledge and awareness of these cultural traits and manifestations are essential in order to orient oneself as a cross-cultural mediator, it is relevant to point out the necessity of a highly developed intercultural sensitivity in order not to fall into the trap of categorising and stereotyping. Individuals may only conform to narrowly defined, culturally determined traits of behaviour and worldviews to a certain degree. As outlined at the beginning, our cultural mobility has increased dramatically and one never knows which personal experiences may have influenced an individual during the course of his/her life. People may have mixed parentage, lived in several countries, or have had defining personal or professional encounters which could have been likely to have had a hybridising effect on their identities; a fact which is important for the intercultural mediator to be mindful of, and sensitive to.

The worldview lies within the language

In Britain, the number of non-native English speakers has been increasing since the 1950s. While 8% of the population belonged to an ethnic minority in 2001, according to a study published in 2010 by the University of Leeds, figures are projected to reach 20% by 2051 (The Guardian, 13.07.2010). Although most immigrants end up learning English one way or another, their language proficiency will ultimately depend on a series of diverse circumstances, which, far from having to do with personal ability alone, imply a number of psycholinguistic factors in which their very own identity plays a crucial role. Language and cultural identity are inextricably linked, a factor which carries multifaceted implications and is often ignored or dismissed by native English-speakers, who take 'English as a universal language' for granted and regard it as the only tool necessary for effective communication with members of other cultures.

According to Granger (2004) we create our social and linguistic self through first language learning. Ting-Toomey (1999) proposes that because it is learned so early in life, language *'permeates the core of our cultural and ethnic identities without our full awarenes of its impact'* (Ting-Toomey, 1999: 92). She further says that

'Language infiltrates so intensely the social experience within a culture that neither language nor culture can be understood without knowledge of both. To understand a culture deeply, we have to understand the culture's language. To understand language in context, we have to understand the fundamental beliefs and value systems that drive particular language usage in particular circumstances' (ibid.: 93).

Jenkins (2003) complements this theory by arguing that cultural aspects which are expressed linguistically, sometimes have no equivalent in other languages and are not translatable. Research conducted by her with assimilated immigrants has shown that, to them, the loss of their cultural language in favour of the dominant language symbolised the loss of their cultural identity.

Relevant to the context of conflict, research conducted by Calhoun (2004), Lutz and Abu-Lughod (1990) has also shown that emotions are equally *'inextricably intertwined with language'* (cited in Leep 2010: 332) and that language choice is often compelled by emotions. Therefore, emotions and language play a big role in expressing one's codified worldview. In an emotionally charged situation, regardless of proficiency levels, it may not always be possible for a foreigner to uphold speaking in a second acquired language (English, in this case). Various reasons may cause linguistic interference i.e., the carrying over of elements from one linguistic system into another. However, in some instances which will be pointed out, due to the strong link between language, culture, identity, and emotions, deeply rooted unconscious reasons may bring a person to avoid his/her native language.

The multiple factors that will be highlighted will demonstrate the need for the mediator to have first, some psycholinguistic understanding, and second, the knowledge of a person's native language in order to be able to deal with the implications which could influence effective communication, and to build a relationship of trust, thus giving the persons in dispute the assurance of being truly heard.

Living between languages

Learning a new language entails taking on a new identity. To a foreigner, the worldview a new language proposes may prove to be difficult to embrace. The resistance to abdicating the identity that he/she considers to be his 'true' one, and to acquiring a 'new self' may persist for a long time. This anxiety of being separated from one's original identity can trigger very strong emotions, as emphasized by Polish author Eva Hoffman (1989) who, in her recount of learning English as an immigrant to Canada, refers to her own vulnerable but powerful sense of reality which she perceives as to be in danger of *'coming under native dominion'* (Hoffman, 1989: 204). This perception makes her defensive and litigious; she fears for her innermost self.

Pavlenko (2005) argues that foreign language speakers feel that their 'emotionally true selves' can only be expressed in their native language, whereas they perceive their affective selves in a foreign language to be fake and artificial. She explains the reason for the difficulty of expressing emotions in a second language in that *'[...] proficiency in emotional expression is not necessarily equivalent to overall language proficiency. Rather, it is mediated by the context of acquisition'* (Pavlenko, 2005: 137). She argues that the ability of affective expression depends on *language embodiment*, which involves a conceptual development received during the language socialization process and affective linguistic conditioning, whereby words and phrases acquire affective connotations through emotionally charged experiences. Therefore Pavlenko concludes that foreign languages are never perceived as embodied since emotion-related words are not integrated with nonverbal sensory representations or autobiographic memories.

However, she argues that the language choice for emotional

expression may not only be determined by what is considered the 'language of the heart', but also by strategic goals, such as social power relations or the speaker's personal needs. One of the reasons that may determine language choice is that a person may feel self-conscious or in a position of lesser power within the social structure when speaking in his/her native tongue in a dominant language setting. Speakers often adopt the speech patterns of their interlocutor for conscious or unconscious needs of social integration.

Aside from social integration, another factor may affect language choice. Unconscious first language rejection may occur because of emotional memory, an association with painful experiences which the individual does not want to allow resurface. This phenomenon was frequently noted by psychologists after WWII, when many German and Jewish immigrants in the US refused to speak German due to the traumatic legacy of the Nazi regime and the Holocaust. The use of a newly acquired language offered them the chance to adopt a new persona. The same phenomenon can be noted by foreign patients in psychoanalysis who communicate with the analyst in a second acquired language. The detachment offered by speaking in an 'emotionally distant' language makes it easier to talk. Often they realize, however, that in order to express certain nuances more precisely, reverting to their mother-tongue tends to trigger much stronger emotions and bring out the core of the issue.

In studying the linguistic behaviour of Japanese-English bilinguals, Jenkins (2003) observed the emotional connotations these speakers perceived in each language world: "My personality changes from Japanese mode to English mode. I'm more sarcastic and joking all the time and outgoing and, well, that's when I'm speaking English. In Japanese, I'm quieter (Eriko)". "I use Japanese when I request something. Japanese is softer ... don't you think so? And when I apologize...well, I might use English if I don't really feel like apologizing. A Japanese apology sounds more sincere (Keiko)" (Jenkins, 2003: 143). These examples show that in cases of individuals who originate from high-context, indirect communication cultures, being able to resort to a language that offers the possibility of more direct and explicit expression may be perceived as a benefit. Pavlenko (2005) illustrates this through the example of Japanese speakers who prefer the use of English to express anger because it is more direct, while in their culture they would only be able to express it indirectly.

An important aspect worth noting in relation to language choice is the fact that it may, in some cases, be misleading and thus provide the possibility of misinterpretation. For consciously or unconsciously driven reasons, a person may also feel compelled to speak in a second language in order to reduce *communicative distance* from the interlocutor. However, in case of a low proficiency level, this attempt of *speech convergence* may not be possible to maintain, causing anxiety in the speaker and hence counteracting effective communication. Pavlenko's (2005) account of research with psychiatric patients is relevant here as it shows that proficiency-related nervousness and anxiety may even result in lack of affect. She argues that the increased attention given to wording, pronounciation and grammar may diminish the attention to the affective component and thus create an inconsistency between the content and the way it is being communicated. The speaker may appear as emotionally withdrawn, detached and less expressive which might be misinterpreted by an inexperienced counsellor. Such occurrences could be transposed to cross-cultural mediation settings, where the ability of the mediator to resort to the speaker's native language could restore the situation and reestablish the necessary trust and empathic understanding.

Another type of linguistic interference is the so-called code-switching, i.e. the switching from one language to another. Bourhis (1979) sustains that this may be affected by the topic of conversation, noting that speakers tend to switch to their native accent, dialect or language when speaking about stressful topics or topics relevant to their worldview. As pointed out before, it is important to recognise that some affective words or expressions do not have an exact equivalent in another language. Pavlenko (2005) argues that although bilinguals manage to categorise and name emotions in their second language, their emotional concepts may not match those of this language's culture, a factor which may also lead to code-switching. She further confirms Bourhis' (1979) argument that the need to code-switch arises from the fact that the first language tends to communicate more intense positive and negative affect and is thus perceived as more emotional. Another reason for code-switching may simply be the low second language proficiency of the speaker.

Silence in cross-cultural mediation

The use of silence is a powerful tool in mediation which is usually applied by the mediator. It needs to be pointed out, however, that in a cross-cultural mediation setting the occurrence of silence may lie outside the mediator's control. Its reasons may come down to a completely different, culturally and linguistically related nature which calls for awareness and proper decoding.

On the cultural side, members of Eastern countries tend to be more comfortable with silence than members of Western countries. For Eastern cultures, silence reduces uncertainty and conveys respect, whereas in the West silence tends to be perceived as uncomfortable, induce anxiety, and convey hostility and disinterest.

On the linguistic side, as mentioned above, the anxiety of a foreign language speaker which relates to identity and self-validation issues, can manifest itself through emotional withdrawal. But it can also be manifested through linguistic withdrawal. Apart from arising because of non-comprehension or as a moment to gather one's lingusitic knowledge, Granger (2004) notes that silence is not limited to absence of verbal expression. It can also be the manifestation of a temporarily lost identity when one's own language or way of speaking loses its validity in the context of a dominant language. Within the present mediation context, it is conceivable that a person might choose to stop speaking in an emotionally charged situation if he/she feels overwhelmed by the anxiety caused by the sensation of not being properly heard. Eva Hoffman's poignant account offers a sense of how it may feel not to be understood: *'Because I'm not heard, I feel I'm not seen'* (Hoffman, 1989: 147). She describes feeling *'impalpable, neutral, faceless'*, as the *'mat look'* in her interlocutor's eyes *'cancel'* her face (ibid.: 147). This situation may not necessarily be proficiency-dependent. It could arise from any of the mentioned instances of high emotional charge and it represents another potential situation that might result in a deadlock. It is trust which is at play, a particularly sensitive question for a foreigner in a dominant culture situation. Again, this could be avoided by the possibility of being able to speak to the mediator in one's first language. By being able to use one's affective language, the anxiety arising from such a situation could be considerably reduced, and the confidence of being understood and truly heard could be upheld or restored.

Co-mediating cross-cultural disputes

From the highlighted aspects above it becomes clear that managing the complexities of one person's worldview and 'language world' is a demanding task. As suggested previously, the co-mediators should ideally come from or be familiar with the culture and language of one of the respective parties. The initial joint session should be kept to outlining the nature of the mediation process and highlighting the rules of the mediation. Details of the conflict are better explored in private sessions with each client before the mediation, while only outlining the nature of the conflict in this joint session, in order to avoid lenghty translations in the case of language incompatibility. It is proposed that each mediator retreats with his/her client into private caucus sessions in which the cultural context contained in the verbal message, in gestures, nonverbal nuances, pauses, and silence is decoded and trust gained. The more culturally distant the parties in dispute are, the more important it is to tend to the parties in these separate caucus sessions in order to create a safe environment for them to disclose the issues and for the mediator to fully understand all the nuances.

Following this and any further exploratory sessions, the mediators should meet and discuss their findings until they uncover common interests and identify any culturally determined obstacles to achieving them. By reporting back to their respective clients, the mediators can raise the awareness of what is mostly the case in cross-cultural disputes, namely that they are based on a mutual lack of awareness of cultural habits and needs. When the right degree of understanding has been achieved, the integration phase can be initiated, whereby constructive and creative solutions can be explored.

Mostly, it comes as a relief to the parties to learn that the underlying problems in the conflict are based on their respective cultural perspectives and not necessarily on ill-will. However, the mediators need to remain aware and mindful of the different negotiation processes between collectivists and individualists, in order to mediate effectively. Particular attention must be given to collectivists' needs for face-saving cooperation and process-oriented negotiation style, as well as to individualists' outcome-oriented style. It remains to be decided by the mediators at which stage of the negotiation process the parties can be safely joined again in order to conclude the negotiation.

Conclusion

The aspects discussed in this chapter highlight that cross-cultural mediation is highly specialised and cannot be conducted effectively without intercultural knowledge and awareness of the multifaceted and complex issues evolving around culturally defined worldviews, including their emotional manifestations and perceptions. What stands out in particular is how fragile and subtle the balancing act becomes when building and maintaining a relationship of trust with a person from another cultural background throughout such a mediation. The points made on affect and language demonstrate that a cross-cultural mediator's linguistic and psycholinguistic knowledge is as important as his/her intercultural skills. Conducting this kind of mediation from a monolingual perspective bears a high potential for deadlock and a breakdown of such trust. Questions of identity and self-value in bilinguals who acquire their second language at a later stage in life are complex and loaded with emotional connotations. They need to be fully understood, not only to convey to the person "I hear what you are saying", but also in order to effectively mediate between the diverging value systems and needs of all the parties involved in the conflict. In a multicultural society, this need calls for the accreditation of interculturally trained foreign native-speakers and highly experienced foreign language speakers to work as mediators in cross-cultural disputes.

References

Apaydin M. (2011) Conference on *The Language of Art and Music* in Berlin, 17-20 February 2011.

Birdwhistell R. (1955) and Mehrabian, A. (1981), cited in: Ting-Toomey, S. 1999.

Communicating Across Cultures New York: Guilford Press. p. 115.

Birdwhistell A. (1970) and Hall, E.T. (1981) cited in: Ting-Toomey, S. 1999. *Communicating Across Cultures* New York: Guilford Press. p. 119.

Bourhis, R.Y., (1979), Language in Ethnic Interaction: A Social Psychological Approach. *IN:* Giles, H. and Saint-Jacques, B. (eds.) '*Language and Ethnic Relations*', Oxford, New York, Toronto, Sydney, Paris, Frankfurt: Pergamon Press. pp. 117 – 141.

Ekman P. and Oster H. (1979) cited in: Ting-Toomey, S. (1999) *Communicating across Cultures*, New York: Guilford Press. p. 115.

Chua, E.G. and Gudykunst, W.B., (1987), *Conflict Resolution Styles in Low and High Context Cultures*, Communication Research Reports, 4, pp. 32-37.

Granger, C., (2004) *Silence in Second Language Learning: A Psychoanalytic Reading*, Clevedon, Buffalo, Toronto, Sydney: Mutilingual Matters.

Hall, E.T., (1976), *Beyond Culture*. New York: Doubleday.

Hasada R. (1997) Some aspects of Japanese cultural ethos embedded in nonverbal communicative behaviour. *IN:* Poyatos, F. (ed.) *'Nonverbal Communication and Translation'*, Amsterdam, Philadelphia: John Benjamins Publishing. p. 83 – 103

Hoffman, E., (1998), *Lost In Translation*. London: Vintage.

Hofstede, G. and Hofstede J.G. (2005), *'Cultures and Organizations: Software of the Mind,'* Revised 2nd ed. New York, Chicago, San Francisco: McGraw Hill.

Jenkins J., (2003), *World Englishes: A resource book for students*, London, New York: Routledge.

Le Baron M., (2002), *Bridging Troubled Waters: Conflict Resolution from the Heart*, San Francisco: Jossey-Bass.

Neuliep, J.W. (2006), *Intercultural Communication: a Contextual Approach*, 3rd ed. Thousand Oaks, London, New Dehli: Sage Publications.

Pavlenko A., (2005), *Emotions and Multilingualism*, Cambridge, New York, Melbourne: Cambridge University Press.

Ting-Toomey, S. (1999). *Communicating Across Cultures*, New York: Guilford Press.

INDEX

GLOSSARY

Bracket	Also called *epoché* or the phenomenological reduction) is a term derived from Edmund Husserl (1859-1938) for the act of suspending judgment about the natural world that precedes phenomenological analysis.
Caucus	A confidential meeting between a disputant party/parties and their mediator/co-mediators
Existential	1. of or relating to existence, esp. human existence 2. (Philosophy) *Philosophy* pertaining to what exists, and is thus known by experience rather than reason; empirical as opposed to theoretical 3. (Philosophy / Logic) *Logic* denoting or relating to a formula or proposition asserting the existence of at least one object fulfilling a given condition; containing an existential quantifier 4. (Philosophy) of or relating to existentialism

Negative introject

> The process of swallowing whole beliefs, attitudes and values of others that when internalized represent 'shoulds, oughts or ought-nots' that prevent us from achieving important personal needs and wants

NLP   Neuro-Linguistic Programming: a stated
       connection between the neurological
       processes ("neuro"), language ("linguistic")
       andbehavioral patterns that have been learned
       through experience ("programming") and can
       be organized to achieve specific goals in life

Noema   That which is directional, '... *the object (the*
       what) that we direct our attention towards and
       focus upon'

Noesis   That which is referential, the 'how' through
       which we define an object.

Projection When parts of the self are split off and
       projected onto an external object or person

Sedimented This is used when a thought, behaviour or
       value gets 'stuck' just as the remains of coffee
       may becomes sedimented and left at the
       bottom of a coffee perculator. They can be
       removed but it takes a little effort.

Transference Intense feelings which a 'patient' [in
       psychotherapy] transfers onto the therapist
       that is neither justified by the therapist's
       behaviour or this situation. This can also
       be understood as the   patient 'acting out'
       experiences from outside the therapy.